WETHERSFIELD INSTITUTE

Proceedings, 1989

THE CATHOLIC WRITER

The Catholic
Writer

Papers Presented at a Conference
sponsored by the Wethersfield Institute
New York City, September 29–30, 1989

EDITED, WITH A PREFACE BY
RALPH McINERNY

IGNATIUS PRESS   SAN FRANCISCO

Cover by Riz Boncan Marsella

©1991 Ignatius Press, San Francisco
ISBN 0–89870–352–2
Library of Congress catalogue number 90–85585
Printed in the United States of America

CONTENTS

THE PROGRAM

CONFERENCE CHAIRMAN

Ralph McInerny
Director, Jacques Maritain Center, University of Notre Dame

SPEAKERS

Russell Hittinger
Assistant Professor of Philosophy, Fordham University
Visiting Professor of Politics, Princeton University

William A. Marra
Professor of Philosophy, Fordham University

Mary Mumbach
Professor of Literature, Thomas More Institute

Michael Novak
American Enterprise Institute, Washington, D.C.

Michael Platt
Middlebury College, Vermont

Joseph Sobran
Senior Editor, *National Review*

Edward A. Synan
The Pontifical Institute of Mediaeval Studies, Toronto

Frederick D. Wilhelmsen
Professor of Philosophy and Politics, University of Dallas,
Irving, Texas

Gregory Wolfe
Editor, *Image: A Journal of the Arts*

WETHERSFIELD INSTITUTE
AWARD RECIPIENT

JAMES FARL POWERS was born in 1917 in Jacksonville, Illinois. From the appearance of his collection of stories *The Prince of Darkness* in 1947, Mr. Powers has been recognized as a writer of consummate skill and profound understanding of the human soul. Almost without exception, his themes and stories have been Catholic, indeed clerical, in nature. *Morte d'Urban,* his first novel, won the National Book Award in 1963 and is undeniably Powers' masterpiece. His second collection of short stories, *The Presence of Grace* (1956), and his third, *See How the Fish Live* (1975), consolidated his reputation as a supreme master of the short story. The long-awaited *Wheat That Springeth Green* was, in the opinion of many, the most important literary event of 1988. Besides the National Book Award, Mr. Powers has received fellowships from the Guggenheim and Rockefeller Foundations. To these honors we are pleased to add the 1989 Wethersfield Institute Award for outstanding literary achievement.

PREFACE

On September 29 and 30, 1989, the Wethersfield Institute sponsored a program on the Catholic writer, one of the main purposes of which was to honor J. F. Powers, who has been for so many of us for so many years the quintessential Catholic writer. The phrase invites controversy, needless to say. Many writers who have been dubbed "Catholic" decline the designation—I think of Graham Greene—while others who accept it do not seem to deal with recognizably Catholic themes—I think of Flannery O'Connor. But whether accepted or rejected, the writer does not want his fiction to be regarded as proselytizing or catechetical. What is the point of the adjective?

Consider a parallel. The Irish writer may be one who just happens to live in Ireland or whose forebears came from there, and the phrase *Catholic writer* could be used in that way, designating any writer who happens to be Catholic. But we would have to be prepared for someone's saying, "Ah, but she isn't really an *Irish* writer, no matter that her mother came from Ireland." And we would understand the point of the demur. Not every Irish writer is an Irish writer. So too, conversely, we understand why, whatever his wishes, Greene will be regarded as a Catholic writer because, given *Brighton Rock, The Labyrinthian Ways, The Heart of the Matter,* and *The End of the Affair,* the designation is inevitable. Evelyn Waugh realized after the fact, when he was preparing the one-volume edition, that in his trilogy *Sword of Honour* he was recording a seismic shift in English Catholicism. Neither writer was out to convert his reader, but the lens through which the events of their novels was told was clearly Catholic, however much they differed from one another.

It is not a matter of having churchy themes or nuns and priests scurrying about: those are sufficient but not necessary reasons for calling fiction Catholic. Indeed, I have come to think

that a case can be made for maintaining that all literature is
Catholic. The case is a bit forced, needless to say, but it would
begin with Flannery O'Connor's contention that all literature —
all literature — must have an anagogic sense. By this she meant
that the actions depicted in the story have a meaning beyond
the temporal realm in which they occur. A person by his fleet-
ing acts, so soon performed, so quickly over, creates a character that lasts, whose import may transcend time. Catholic? One
could argue that this is a fundamental assumption of Western
literature. Actions matter because men are free and responsible for what they do. The Catholic lens is merely a special instance of this grand assumption that permeates Homer and
Aeschylus and Virgil as well as Christian writers.

For purposes of the Wethersfield Conference, we were of
course content to select acknowledged instances of the Catholic
writer. We did not first define the category and then look for
writers to fit it. The analysis has to go in just the opposite direction. Gregory Wolfe was given the task of setting the tone for
the program, and he did so magnificently. We then proceeded
to talks on Hilaire Belloc, Gilbert Keith Chesterton, and Flannery O'Connor. Nor did we confine ourselves to imaginative
writers. Christopher Dawson, Dietrich von Hildebrand, Jacques Maritain, and Étienne Gilson received masterful treatment.
Of course, it is easier to decide whether a philosopher or historian is Catholic.

A special word about Michael Platt's piece on Willa Cather.
If we had worked with an a priori and narrow notion of the
Catholic writer, it would have been absurd to include it. In
the case of Willa Cather, one could have argued from *Death
Comes for the Archbishop*. But I prefer to let the significant portion of Platt's talk printed here provide its own justification
for inclusion.

J. F. Powers honored us with his presence throughout the
conference and suffered through the praise heaped upon him
at the banquet. Printed on page twelve is the citation read

when he was presented with the Wethersfield Award. If the notion of Catholic writer is analogous, J. F. Powers could well serve as the primary analogate.

Special thanks to Edmée de Montmollin and Alice Osberger, two *sine quibus non* of the conference.

Ralph McInerny

PRESENTATION OF THE
WETHERSFIELD AWARD
SEPTEMBER 29, 1989

On this feast of the holy angels Michael, Raphael, and Gabriel, we meet to do honor to an author whose first book was called *The Prince of Darkness*. His keen and mordant eye has found flaws and foibles in the Order of Melchizedek but has always seen as well *The Presence of Grace*. *Morte d'Urban*, with its haunting quotation from Barrie, "The life of every man is a diary in which he means to write one story and writes another", put an ironic Christian spin on its hero's motto, "Be a winner!" Totally immersed in his subject, he next invited us to *See How the Fish Live*. During more than thirty years, he has been recognized as a major American writer, a craftsman without peer, an author whose stories are universal because they are so particular, a Catholic whose voice is music to the secular ear as well as to those of his coreligionists. Last year, in *Wheat That Springeth Green*, he showed himself to be at the height of his powers, an elevation reached by few other writers. For his wisdom and wit, for his art and faith, for the stories he has told and those he has yet to tell, the Wethersfield Institute is proud to bestow its award for outstanding literary achievement on JAMES FARL POWERS.

GREGORY WOLFE

"EVER ANCIENT, EVER NEW":
THE CATHOLIC WRITER
IN THE MODERN WORLD

The . . . tradition [of Christian culture] exists today, for though
the Church no longer inspires and dominates the external culture of the modern world, it still remains the guardian of all the
riches of its own inner life. . . . If society were once again Christian . . . this sacred tradition would once more flow out into the
world and fertilize the culture of societies yet unborn. Thus the
movement toward Christian culture is at one and the same time
a voyage into the unknown, in the course of which new worlds
of human experience will be discovered, and a return to our own
fatherland—to the sacred tradition of the Christian past which
flows underneath the streets and cinemas and skyscrapers of the
new Babylon as the tradition of patriarchs and prophets flowed
beneath the palaces and amphitheaters of Imperial Rome.[1]

Whenever I have had the chance to visit second-hand book-
shops in recent years—whether they be converted barns in
Pennsylvania, decaying mansions in the Corktown section of
Detroit, or dank corridors in Oxford or London—I have found
myself shouting out my discoveries to my friends. More often
than not, my finds have been books by Catholic thinkers that
have been out of print for twenty or thirty years. On their
frayed dust jackets and faded paper covers, the praise of critics
whose names are all but forgotten today testifies to the excite-
ment these books once generated. The prices have been hard
to beat: Romano Guardini's *The End of the Modern World* for
a dollar, Christopher Dawson's *The Historic Reality of Christian
Culture* for 30 pence, Chesterton's *Manalive* for a quarter. Many

of these books come from libraries—predominantly Catholic libraries. In fact, I have personally profited from the closing of dozens of seminaries and convents in the Anglo-American world. With a feeling that is at once elated and guilty, I run off with spoils that once lined the shelves of imposing Gothic buildings.

In reflecting upon the topic of this conference, it occurred to me that my book-hunting adventures might serve as a metaphor for the sweeping changes in Catholic intellectual and cultural life over the last twenty-five years. The writers whose works I was collecting were those who constituted what was once called the Catholic Intellectual Renaissance, an outpouring of philosophy, theology, history, and literature which combined fidelity to the ancient teachings of the Church with considerable sophistication of mind and spirit. Here were the works of the minds who dominated Catholic letters for the first half of the twentieth century, gathering dust, rejected by the current establishment, only to be discovered and then hoarded as treasures by a small segment of the younger generation.

The outstanding Catholic historian James Hitchcock has termed the eclipse of these writers in the 1960s and 1970s "the slaying of the fathers".[2] But in cocktail parties at most Catholic universities today, the mention of names such as Maritain, Gilson, Mauriac, or Waugh would very likely evoke not so much hostility as an amused condescension for individuals who are considered thoroughly passé. Relegated to that zone of weeping and gnashing of teeth known as the "pre–Vatican II" world, the Maritains and Mauriacs are thought of as apologists for an order that has been largely left behind in our progress toward a more enlightened dispensation. "To be sure," the cocktail chat might go, "they were men of cultivation and learning, even of wit, but, you know, they were positively *medieval.*"

Of course, many of the writers of the Catholic Renaissance would have been flattered to be associated with the Middle Ages, a time which to them connoted not barbaric darkness but a remarkably integrated culture, a world of light and grace,

where flesh and spirit jointly mounted toward heaven. But leaving the virtues of the High Middle Ages aside for the moment,
I would like to suggest that, in the long run, the thinkers who
made up the Catholic Renaissance will prove to be the most
authentically modern and original of all. Scratch a progressive
and more often than not you will find, just beneath the language of "liberation" and "dialogue", notions that made their
first appearance during the debates of the patristic era. But show
me a thinker who has faithfully grappled with the achievements
of Saint Augustine or Saint Thomas, and you will likely find
someone who has the ability to grasp the real challenges of the
modern world.

As will be evident by now, I am pursuing a paradox about
the spiritual and intellectual life of the Church. Chesterton, that
modern master of paradox, has come very close to the matter
in his discussion of the term *reform*. For Chesterton, the word
reform is both meaningless and dangerous unless we recover
its literal definition. The liberal conceptions of reform as either
a gradual evolution away from an older doctrine or practice
or as a revolution against tradition are woefully misguided.
True reform, he says, involves a return to *form*. Only in sub-
jecting oneself to the rigors of the original form—a term that
itself reminds us of something ordered, coherent, and specific—
can the detritus of time and human folly be washed away and
vitality return.

But just as one might step in at this point and argue that
Chesterton's definition is really nothing more than a slavish
imitation of the past, notice how the paradox executes its boom-
erang turn. By returning to the original form from the stand-
point of the crisis of the present, the resulting reform might
well take on a radically different path when compared with the
immediate past. In other words, the return to form may yield
results that are startling but that remain true both to the distant past and to the conditions of the present. (Chesterton loved
his self-proclaimed role as a "conservative radical".) As the bril-
liant theologian Cardinal Henri de Lubac puts it in his *Paradoxes*

of Faith: "To get away from old things passing themselves off
as tradition it is necessary to go back to the farthest past—
which will reveal itself to be the nearest present."[3]

Beyond the paradoxes of intellectual history and institutional
reform, of course, lies the fundamental paradox of the divine
nature itself, which Saint Augustine described as the beauty that
is "ever ancient, ever new".[4] It is also the paradox of the Gospels, which remain united with the Old Testament even while
ushering in the New. The thinkers we group under the heading of the Catholic Intellectual Renaissance embodied that paradox in their writing. It is what makes them at the same time
profoundly traditional and strikingly modern. Few of these
figures could be called tame or timid; ever the servants of the
Church, they nonetheless were bold, occasionally shocking,
figures, who were suspected by some of their less imaginative
contemporaries of being imprudent or even heretical. At times,
the accusations of the superorthodox led to excruciatingly bi-
zarre situations, as when Evelyn Waugh, that staunchest of
papal Catholics, was accused by a prominent priest-editor of
writing a novel that would corrupt the morals of the faithful.
Waugh's long letter of justification to the archbishop of Westminster, with its patient explanation of his harshly ironic satire
against modern secularism, makes for grimly comic reading.[5]
But these attacks from the extreme Right balance those of the
Left and offer further proof of the wisdom and vision of these
great minds.

The Catholic Intellectual Renaissance

It is not possible within the scope of this presentation to give
an historical account of the origins of the Catholic Intellectual
Renaissance and its influence on modern thought. After a brief
sketch of some of the key features of the Renaissance, I will
outline three major themes which to me represent some of the

greatest achievements of these writers and will conclude with
a reflection on their relevance for the present.

In theology, there is a principle which states that the bigger
and more mysterious a being is, metaphysically speaking, the
harder it is to describe its nature in direct terms. When it comes
to understanding God himself, it has often been said that it is
better to attempt to say what he is not, and in this way inch
closer to a perception of what he is. I would like to borrow
this technique to describe the modern Catholic Renaissance.
First, the Renaissance was not an expression of anything that
might be called an "establishment". The single most striking
fact about the majority of its writers is that they were converts.
In the earlier generation, one could point out Léon Bloy, Jacques and Raïssa Maritain, Paul Claudel, Gabriel Marcel, Charles
Péguy, Evelyn Waugh, Graham Greene, Christopher Dawson,
G. K. Chesterton, Ronald Knox, Edith Stein, and Adrienne von
Speyr. The younger generation included such converts as Louis
Bouyer and Walker Percy. Add to this such near-converts as
Henri Bergson and Simone Weil, as well as the Anglo-Catholic
converts T. S. Eliot and W. H. Auden, and you have a picture
of a worldview that had the capacity to draw many of the lead-
ing minds of the age.

Conversion is an experience that is in some sense unique to
every convert, but it inevitably involves a process of discovery—the feeling, to quote T. S. Eliot, of arriving home and
knowing the place for the first time. Ironically, many of these
intellectual converts did not find ready acceptance in official
ecclesiastical circles. All this goes to show that the converts were
hardly submitting themselves blindly to authority figures in
order to assuage their anxieties about sex, guilt, and death (a
common charge of their secular critics). Rather, they were engaged in a protracted mental and spiritual struggle that ended
in a willing embrace of the central mysteries of the Faith. To
all of them, their faith was an asset, a key to understanding
both the highest truths and the most pressing problems of the

moment. They would undoubtedly share Flannery O'Connor's belief that "there is no reason why fixed dogma should fix anything that the writer sees in the world. On the contrary, dogma is an instrument for penetrating reality. Christian dogma is about the only thing left in the world that surely guards and respects mystery."[6]

If the Renaissance intellectuals were not creatures of any establishment, neither did they form a "movement". There were, of course, "schools" of thought, including the Thomists, the Catholic existentialists, and the neo-patristic theologians, but even within these schools there were widely divergent views. This point may seem a truism, but it is, to my mind, an important corroboration of the intellectual honesty of these thinkers that, while they shared a common faith, their explorations of the world took them down disparate paths.

Finally, it is worth noting that these writers were predominantly laypeople, not clerics. We take the leadership of lay intellectuals in the Church today somewhat for granted, but it has largely been a modern development. It is a development that recent popes and the Second Vatican Council itself have strongly endorsed, seeing it as a necessary consequence of an increasingly secularized society, and also because the specific character of the laity is to know the natural goods of various forms of worldly endeavor. The leading figures of the Catholic Renaissance moved easily and naturally in secular professional circles — a fact we may tend to forget. This is a testament not only to the greater openness of secular intellectuals in the earlier decades of the century but also to their positive rejection of the fortress mentality on the part of the Renaissance thinkers. Their place, as they saw it, was on the front lines of culture, and if they encountered some hostility, they also found a great deal of respect. As James Hitchcock has pointed out, the Catholic Thomists helped to spur a neo-scholastic movement that was taken up by such teachers as Mortimer Adler and Richard McKeon at the University of Chicago, where the joke was that "atheist professors taught Catholic philosophy to Jewish students."[7]

It has been said that orthodoxy develops only in response to the challenges posed by heresy. But if the great orthodox thinkers have received their impetus from the need to oppose a narrowing and distortion of the faith, it is equally true that they always manage to rise above merely defensive postures to achieve a vision which reawakens in us a sense of the beauty and wonder of the world. One need only think of a work like Saint Augustine's *The City of God,* which was written as a response to the pagans who claimed that Christianity was responsible for the fall of the Roman Empire. This magisterial book not only refuted those charges but became the blueprint for the political and social order of medieval Europe for nearly a millennium. I would like to suggest that the greatest of the Catholic Renaissance writers in the modern era accomplished this twofold mission of critique and imaginative vision. Of the many themes that run throughout their writings, I have chosen to single out three: the recovery of the sacred, the critique of the world, and the assimilation of modernity.

The Recovery of the Sacred

In the age dominated by Darwin, Marx, and Freud, human nature appeared to be determined by evolution, the means of production, or the unconscious, or, in the case of a few creative scholars, a combination of these forces. Few of the thinkers of the Catholic Renaissance dismissed entirely the insights into the workings of the mind and the social order that came in the wake of modern psychology, sociology, and natural science. Catholic existentialists like Gabriel Marcel adapted the Freudian and Sartrean notions of alienation, but he placed them in the context of the traditional Christian understanding of man as a stranger and pilgrim on the earth. Marcel preferred to speak of *Homo Viator,* Man the Wayfarer.

Like Marcel, the Renaissance writers retained the conviction that man's life, far from being mechanically determined, is in-

herently dramatic, poised between sin and grace. It should come
as no surprise that the Catholic novelist was in a particularly
strong position to reawaken the transcendent dimension of human experience. As Flannery O'Connor put it:

> Drama usually bases itself on the bedrock of original sin, whether
> the writer thinks in theological terms or not. . . . The novelist
> doesn't write about people in a vacuum; he writes about people
> in a world where something is obviously lacking, where there
> is the general mystery of incompleteness and the particular
> tragedy of our own times to be demonstrated and the novelist
> tries to give you, within the form of the book, a total experi-
> ence of human nature at any time. For this reason the greatest
> dramas naturally involve the salvation or loss of the soul. When
> there is no belief in the soul, there is very little drama.[8]

Where the Catholic novelists of the twentieth century have
succeeded in providing us with intimations of grace, they have
revealed it in experiences that seem to confound our normal
expectations for revelation. Greene, Mauriac, Bernanos, and
O'Connor, among others, have depicted grace in the lives of
seemingly odious and pitiful individuals, in moments of violence, and in quiet, almost unnoticeable ways. Though these
novelists were accused of being obsessed by dark visions of
sin, they replied that grace is precisely an irruption of the divine into the fallen creation.

Evelyn Waugh is a case in point. Known primarily for his
biting satire, Waugh, in *Brideshead Revisited,* set himself the am-
bitious goal of showing "the operation of divine grace on a
group of diverse but closely connected characters".[9] Ironically,
the reaction of many readers, including a good number of Catholics, to *Brideshead* can be summarized by a letter Waugh received from an American reader soon after its publication:
"Your *Brideshead Revisited* is a strange way to show that Catholicism is an answer to anything. Seems more like the kiss of
Death."[10] A plot summary would certainly seem to support
that contention. The agnostic painter Charles Ryder witnesses

one member after another of the Catholic, aristocratic Flyte family die or fade away in lives that appear largely futile. Early in the novel, Ryder's intimate friend Sebastian Flyte explains:

> So you see we're a mixed family religiously. Brideshead and Cordelia are both fervent Catholics; he's miserable, she's bird-happy; Julia and I are half-heathen; I am happy, I rather think Julia isn't; Mommy is popularly believed to be a saint and Papa is excommunicated — and I wouldn't know which of them was happy. Anyway, however you look at it, happiness doesn't seem to have much to do with it, and that's all I want . . . I wish I liked Catholics more.[11]

By the end of the novel, Sebastian and Cordelia are also living stunted and sad lives. But, as happens so often in the fiction of Evelyn Waugh, a throwaway phrase contains the core of the novel's meaning: "happiness doesn't seem to have much to do with it".

For Waugh, the notion that the life of faith ought to lead inevitably to worldly prosperity and what the pop psychologists call "wellness" is both unrealistic and dangerous. In a fallen world, afflicted by evil and stupidity, happiness can never be a gauge of fidelity to God. To think otherwise is to confuse happiness, with its bourgeois connotations of comfort and freedom from any burdens, with *blessedness,* or what Catholics call the "state of grace".

Catholics, Waugh believed, have always clung to the foot of the cross, profoundly and intuitively aware of what the Spanish philosopher Unamuno called "the tragic sense of life". When Julia Flyte, one of the "half-heathens", reaches a moment of crisis in *Brideshead Revisited,* it is the unexpected memory of the crucifix on the wall of her nursery that shocks her into a recognition of how far she has drifted from God. As the characters in *Brideshead* enact their "fierce little human tragedy", it becomes clear that they are all in some fashion struggling against God and his Church, symbolized by Brideshead Castle, that magnificent baroque backdrop to the novel's action. Thomas Howard has spoken of the Church as the "unseen" character in the novel.

I am convinced that Waugh intended the Church to look like the "kiss of death", not out of perversity but because he understood it to be a "sign of contradiction". The sufferings that it seemingly inflicts, because of its laws and absolute claims, are the bitter herbs through which the disease of sin is purged. On closer inspection, the lives that the characters lead at the end of the novel, while not "happy", are in many ways "blessed". Sebastian is a holy fool, a drunken porter for a monastery in North Africa. When he learns of this, Charles asks Cordelia: "I suppose he doesn't suffer?"

> Oh yes, I think he does. One can have no idea what the suffering might be, to be maimed as he is — no dignity, no power of will. No one is ever holy without suffering. It's taken that form with him. . . . I've seen so much suffering in the last few years; there's so much of it coming for everybody soon. It's the spring of love.[12]

Brideshead Revisited is only one example of the ways in which the twentieth-century Catholic writers sought to recover the sense of the sacred. But in its depiction of the Church as a sign of contradiction, it fulfills Flannery O'Connor's requirements of revealing both a drama of salvation and a way of addressing "the particular tragedy of our own times".

The Critique of the World

The second theme, which I call "the critique of the world", is, admittedly, broad and amorphous. What I wish to focus on is the fact that Catholicism reminds us that we can never allow ourselves to become too closely identified with the order of worldly goods. I have chosen to focus on a less frequently discussed theme, namely, the association of Christianity with bourgeois materialism in the modern age, but I could just have

easily explored the Christian critique of totalitarianism, as in
Solzhenitsyn, or the reemergence of gnosticism.

We are told in the Gospels to be in the world but not of it.
From the time of the apostles down to the present, the tension between "Christ and Culture", as the Protestant theologian
H. Richard Niebuhr has put it, has remained constant. The
writers of the Catholic Renaissance faced strong challenges from
modern novelists and political philosophers who accused Christianity of being nothing more than a prop for a decadent bour-
geoisie. Philosophers as different as Kierkegaard and Nietzsche
had railed against a complacent, bourgeois Christianity in the
nineteenth century, and in the twentieth, novelists like James
Joyce and D. H. Lawrence portrayed organized religion as
hypocritical, repressive, and out of touch with human needs.
Despite attempts to declare such writers anti-Christian, their
depictions carried the conviction of experience and cannot be
dismissed.

Catholic social thought, both in the tradition of papal encyc-
licals and in the works of Renaissance scholars such as Jacques
Maritain, Yves Simon, and, in a later generation, John Court-
ney Murray, steered a middle course between the extremes of
radical capitalism and revolutionary socialism. Stressing the importance of a recovery of the notion of the common good, these
thinkers avoided baptizing any current political system. In this
sense, they followed the wisdom of returning to form—that
is, to the Augustinian understanding of the tension between
the City of God and the City of Man—in order to achieve true
reform.

If the problem of a too ready identification between Christian values and the bourgois life seems less applicable to contemporary Europe, it certainly retains its bite for America in
the 1990s. Despite our secularized public institutions, America
is a nation awash in religion and religious expression. But
American Christianity has always suffered from a chameleon-
like tendency to become identified with civil religion and popu-

lar culture. From the gospel of success preached by certain
strains of fundamentalists, to the New Age pantheism that
characterizes much of progressive Catholic thought these days,
the Faith is often of the world but not quite in it, if I may be
permitted to reverse the metaphor.

Once again, I would like to draw my illustration from the
thing I know best, literature. The French Catholic novelists —
Léon Bloy, François Mauriac, and Georges Bernanos — succeeded in continuing the tradition of the fictional critique of
bourgeois society which had been pioneered by Gustave Flaubert and Émile Zola. But whereas Flaubert could only see
Christianity as a beautiful dream that had been corrupted by
complacency and provincialism, the Catholic novelists managed
to depict the same symptoms while preserving a vision of the
radical transcendence of true faith.

François Mauriac's *Viper's Tangle* appears to stack the decks
against Christianity. Written in the form of a diary, it is the
testimony of a lawyer named Louis, who quickly reveals himself to be a thoroughly nasty figure — a moral monster, in fact.
Nearing death, Louis is a peasant who has risen in the world,
becoming a wealthy landowner. Estranged from his wife for
over forty years, and possessed of a loathing for his children,
Louis masterminds a scheme to disinherit his family, which,
he thinks, waits like a pack of vultures to descend on his car-
cass and divide up his fortune.

Louis frankly confesses to being a hate-filled man. One of
his abiding hatreds is for religion itself. Part of this stems
from his upbringing. Louis' mother represents the kind of
smugness to which the peasant mind is often prone. "My
mother never talked to me about religion, except to say — 'I
am quite easy in my mind: if people like ourselves are not
saved, then nobody will be.'"[13] His wife, who comes from
a higher social plane, maintains a piety that he finds maudlin
and superstitious.

But one fact about Louis soon becomes evident: "I have never
possessed the power of self-deception which is most men's

stand-by in the struggle for existence. When I have acted basely, I have always known precisely what I was doing."[14] Indeed, Louis' caustic comments about the world around him are often true; he has a remarkable capacity for sensing hypocrisy and, in a word, sinfulness. In his negation, he often hits targets that deserve to be hit.

As his confessions proceed—for that is what they really are—chinks in Louis's misanthropic armor begin to appear. His plot eventually breaks down, and the dream of revenge which he had nursed for so many years leaves him vulnerable. His wife dies, without any real reconciliation between them, and he discovers among her papers evidence that her shallow piety had deepened into a sacrificial, even ascetic, form of suffering. He realizes that the one thing he had deceived himself about all these years is his need for love, human and divine love. Just before he dies, he accepts what he once called the "sublime lunacies" of Christianity.

In summary form, the plot of *Viper's Tangle* will hardly sound convincing. But the underlying irony of the novel is that, contrary to everyone's assumptions, Louis is driven not by the love of money, which he uses merely as a form of insulation, but by a hunger for the absolute. What separates Louis from most of those around him is that he is not lukewarm; his very coldness contains within it the possibility for reversal. The intensity of his desire for something more than riches becomes his path to salvation. Ironically, the book ends with a letter from his son, who plans to use his inherited wealth by investing in a cinema and a new liqueur—the two symbolic drugs of the modern materialist world. Only a niece recognizes that Louis was "the only truly religious person I have ever met".[15]

François Mauriac's astringent vision offers little comfort to those who seek uplift from art with religious themes, but his lack of sentimentality is precisely what makes him a master of what Flannery O'Connor called "Christian realism". His depiction of a restless heart is a powerful indictment of culture which has lost touch with the demands of supernatural faith.

The Assimilation of Modernity

The final theme I want to touch upon may appear to be another truism. It is simply this: that these twentieth-century Catholic writers were, in fact, modern men, and that they participated fully in the unique opportunities and difficulties of the modern world. It is worth saying because, among those who consider themselves orthodox, there is a persistent tendency toward nostalgia and a provincialism that brands everything "modern" as decadent, or even demonic. Flannery O'Connor once said that "smugness is the Great Catholic Sin",[16] one to which we are all prone. Cardinal de Lubac puts it this way: "'Know the moderns in order to answer their difficulties and their expectations.' A touching intention. But this way of projecting the 'moderns' into an objective concept, of separating oneself from them to consider them from the outside, makes this good will useless."[17]

The Church, because it embraces the truth about human nature and human destiny, has always been able to assimilate new ideas and new cultural patterns, finding in them redemptive possibilities. To quote Cardinal de Lubac again:

> No longer to believe, in fact, in the assimilating and transforming power of Christianity; to divert the exercise of Christian prudence so as to make of it an entirely negative and defensive prudential system: such is one of the most fatal forms of lack of faith. It is to believe no longer, in fact, in Christian vitality. It is to refuse confidence in the Holy Spirit. It is to justify as if on principle those who think that Christianity has grown old for good.[18]

The leading figures of the Catholic Renaissance did not think this way. Philosophers such as Gabriel Marcel and Dietrich von Hildebrand established a healthy dialogue with existentialism and phenomenology, respectively. The painter Georges Rouault drew inspiration from the fauvist and expressionist movements in art. Even Chesterton, seemingly the most defiantly anachronistic of writers, employed Joycean literary techniques in *The Man Who Was Thursday* to convey the chaos of modern subjectivism. An apt illustration of this assimilative capacity is the aesthetic theory of this century's two leading Thomists, Jacques Maritain and Étienne Gilson. Cultivated and urbane scholars, these men devoted a large portion of their philosophical study to aesthetics. Throughout their careers, they asserted that an appreciation of works of the imagination is essential to the fulfillment of our humanity. Both were unabashed champions of modern art. Maritain maintained a close personal friendship with Rouault; his wife, Raïssa, was a poet. Gilson's daughter Jacqueline was a painter in the semiabstract style.

In their description of the history of art, Maritain and Gilson claimed, contrary to most people's intuition, that painting began to go downhill after Giotto "discovered" perspective and ushered in the era of representational painting, and only began to recover with Cézanne and the revolution of modern art. The reason for this hinges on the definition of the purpose of art. The common belief is that art should be an *imitation* of reality, rendered with a faithfulness that approaches that of the camera. But Maritain and Gilson countered that the end of art is not the mere repetition of reality through imitation but the creation of beautiful objects that enable us to see through nature to deeper meaning. No artist creates pure representations of reality: we tend to admire artists precisely insofar as they possess a unique style that moves away from imitation and communicates a penetrating vision of reality.

Gilson's difficult but rewarding book *Painting and Reality* (the Mellon Lectures of 1955) contains this explanation:

> During the long episode that lasted from the end of the fifteenth century to the beginning of the nonpresentational art, painters, instead of remaining firmly established on the ground of nature, progressively or regressively shifted over to the ground of imitation, representation, and, in short, exchanged making for knowing. Imitation—that is, representation of reality as it appears to

be — stands on the side of science or, to use a more modest word, knowledge. Reduced to its simplest expression, the function of modern art has been to restore painting to its primitive and true function, which is to continue through man the creative activity of nature. In so doing modern painting has destroyed nothing and condemned nothing that belongs in any one of the legitimate activities of man; it has simply regained the clear awareness of its own nature and recovered its own place among the creative activities of man.[19]

Based on this line of reasoning, it should come as no surprise that Gilson was also a champion of abstraction, that form of art which so many people assume to be the expression of nihilism and despair about human life. Gilson's use of the word *primitive* is not accidental either: the modernist painters deliberately returned to primitive cave paintings and tribal masks in order to recover a sense of the mythical and sacred in the midst of an industrial, bourgeois society. Rouault went back to the naive representations of medieval stained glass in his struggle to convey man's spiritual destiny. Great artists have always known that the need to attain freshness and vitality can only be achieved by returning to the farthest past, which, as de Lubac reminds us, "will reveal itself to be the nearest present".

The creation of beautiful objects, for their own sake, Gilson insists, is a direct analogy to the creative power of God. Of course, man cannot create something out of nothing, but in making new "beings", the artist "will know the exhilarating feeling of finding himself in contact with the closest analogue there is, in human experience, to the creative power from which all the beauties of art as well as those of nature ultimately proceed. Its name is Being."[20]

The Relevance of the Renaissance Writers

What, then, is the relevance of the writers of the Catholic Intellectual Renaissance to the present, and to the future? As the twentieth century draws to a close, our situation as Catholics seems even more perilous and uncertain than in the heyday of these thinkers. The Church has been plunged into a crisis of identity and confidence in the upheaval that followed the Second Vatican Council. Those who wish to defend the Faith may naturally feel that in the present we do not have the luxury for novels, paintings, and works of scholarship. Understandably, there is a drive toward activism, to the launching of sorties from a well-defended fortress into the hostile territory of secular culture.

What would these writers advise us to do, were they here today? Though many of them expressed deep concern near the ends of their lives about the direction of certain movements in the Church, I am convinced that they would counsel us to do just as they did. They would exhort us to have confidence in God's providence, to reach back into the richness of our tradition and find ways to apply it to the present. In the words of the Dominican writer Gerald Vann:

> It is for us Christians, then . . . to do these two things. First, to learn to be receptive of life before plunging into activity; to learn to be possessed of life, of truth, of love, to be possessed by God. Then secondly, to learn to face the squalors of life as they come to us—and we do not grow into the light by trying to escape the darkness but by meeting it—with courage and tranquility, as we shall then be enabled to do; trying to make sure that the deeper our knowledge of it becomes, the deeper also becomes our sense of oneness with the redemptive pity of God, and therefore the less our danger of coming to terms with evil . . . . In that way we shall incidentally integrate ourselves; for we shall find that, in a world which is so largely uncreative and so largely hopeless, we for our part shall find always a renewal of life and of hope, through our sharing, however humbly, however fumblingly and imperfectly, in the re-creative, the redemptive, work of the Word who was made flesh and dwelt amongst us in order precisely that we might have life and have it more abundantly.[21]

In short, our task is to redeem the time, to be inspired by the One who said: "Behold, I make all things new."

NOTES

[1] Christopher Dawson, *The Reality of Christian Culture* (London: Routledge & Kegan Paul, 1960), pp. 29–30.

[2] James Hitchcock, "Post-Mortem on a Rebirth: The Catholic Intellectual Renaissance", in *Years of Crisis: Collected Essays, 1970–1983* (San Francisco: Ignatius Press, 1987), p. 116.

[3] Henri de Lubac, *Paradoxes of Faith* (San Francisco: Ignatius Press, 1987), p. 20.

[4] Saint Augustine, *Confessions*, X.27.

[5] Evelyn Waugh, "An Open Letter to the Archbishop of Westminster", in *The Letters of Evelyn Waugh*, ed. Mark Amory (Harmondsworth, England: Penguin, 1982), pp. 72–78.

[6] Flannery O'Connor, *Mystery and Manners* (London: Faber & Faber, 1972), p. 178.

[7] Hitchcock, *Years of Crisis*, p. 107.

[8] O'Connor, *Mystery and Manners*, p. 167.

[9] My discussion of *Brideshead Revisited* is based on my essay "Evelyn Waugh: Savage Indignation", in the forthcoming book *The Reality and the Vision* (Waco, Tex.: Word Books, 1990).

[10] *The Essays, Articles, and Reviews of Evelyn Waugh* (Boston: Little, Brown, 1983), p. 304.

[11] Evelyn Waugh, *Brideshead Revisited* (Boston: Little, Brown, 1945), p. 89.

[12] Ibid., p. 309.

[13] François Mauriac, *Viper's Tangle* (New York: Carroll & Graf, 1987), p. 28.

[14] Ibid., p. 17.

[15] Ibid., pp. 204–5.

[16] Flannery O'Connor, *The Habit of Being* (New York: Farrar, Straus & Giroux, 1979), p. 131.

[17] de Lubac, *Paradoxes of Faith*, p. 47.

[18] Ibid., p. 144.

[19] Étienne Gilson, *Painting and Reality* (New York: Meridian Books, 1959), p. 264.

[20] Ibid., p. 275.

[21] Gerald Vann, *Modern Culture and Christian Renewal* (Washington, D.C.: Thomist Press, 1965), pp. 28–29.

RUSSELL HITTINGER

CHRISTOPHER DAWSON:
A VIEW FROM THE SOCIAL SCIENCES

I

In his keynote address to this conference, Gregory Wolfe has
summarized some of the main themes of the Catholic Intellec-
tual Renaissance of this century. He noted that the Renaissance
was led by converts: in France, the Maritains, Paul Claudel,
Léon Bloy, Charles Péguy, and Gabriel Marcel; in England,
G. K. Chesterton, Christopher Dawson, Ronald Knox, Graham
Greene, Evelyn Waugh, and the Anglo-Catholic converts T.
S. Eliot and C. S. Lewis; in America, Allen Tate and his wife,
Caroline Gordon, Thomas Merton, Walker Percy, and Robert
Lowell. This comprises only a short list of prominent converts
who distinguished themselves as intellectuals and who made
it easier for other Catholics to reaffirm the integrity of the life
of faith and reason.

If we put Christopher Dawson in the context of the twentieth-century Intellectual Renaissance, he was different from
the other great lights by virtue of the fact that he was not a
poet, a philosopher, or a theologian. Generally speaking, those
involved in this Intellectual Renaissance excelled and made contributions in three areas:

1. They made contributions in the *literary-aesthetic* area. Indeed,
it would seem that this was the main field of achievement, especially for the converts. Why this was so is an interesting question, which I shall not expand upon in any detail here, except
to say that it was probably due, in part, to what remained of

nineteenth-century literary culture, which elevated the poet to a position equal to that of the scientist — a status we now afford only to entertainers and sports celebrities. Literary modernism was perhaps the only species of modernism that encouraged second thoughts about the moral and spiritual health of modern culture.

2. Impressive contributions were made, as I already mentioned, in *philosophy*. Some believed at the time that the philosophers were given too much credit — especially by Church authorities — and arrogated to themselves the privilege of judging what was intellectually fit or unfit for Catholics. There is a story, probably apocryphal, that has Raïssa Maritain asking a woman, "Are you a Thomist?" "No, but I'm a Catholic." "Well, at least that's a start."[1] We are probably still too close to the period to appreciate the success of the Leonine Revival — the revival of scholastic philosophy and theology prompted by Pope Leo XIII's encyclical *Aeterni Patris* (1879).

3. Finally, there was the area of *theology*, in which clerics in particular excelled: Danielieu, de Lubac, von Balthasar, Rahner, and a host of lesser lights who would still be far superior to anyone we have today; Cardinal Ratzinger represents one of the last of that generation. In this area, it is clear why clerics predominated; for this was before the days when laymen took seminary courses; and theology courses taught in Catholic colleges were primarily catechetical. Simply put, there was no institutional context for raising up a cadre of lay theologians. I do not believe any of us will live to see that happen in our day. To produce a theologian like Rahner or von Balthasar requires decades of preparation in languages, philosophy, and historical studies. I know of no seminary or secular university in the world that reproduces educationally what the Jesuits of a generation ago routinely gave to their brighter men by the time of ordination. The gestation period for high-grade theological work is perhaps too long for contemporary culture.

Apologists like Chesterton and C. S. Lewis, of course, combined all three of these specialties.

Dawson was an exception to this pattern because he was a social scientist. And this should give us pause, for the miscellany of subjects and methods drawn together under the rubric "social science" represents something very close to the core of the modern mind. In any of the other disciplines, one will find premodern examples: there is an obvious relation between Aristotle, Descartes, and Newton, just as there is between Homer, Virgil, Dante, and the modern Welsh poet David Jones. I am not sure that this is true (except by the most extenuated analogy) for sociology. In other words, that Dawson stood alone in this field suggests to me that the Catholic Renaissance was an incomplete intellectual response to modernity. Indeed, I want to suggest (for to treat this at its proper level of detail is beyond the bounds of what I am prepared to do here) that this incompleteness explains why, in our day, the social sciences moved into Catholicism like so many bacteria for which we had no immune system. While Catholics were prepared to deal, for example, with Kantian epistemology, or modern critical methods in biblical studies, or literary modernism, they were not prepared to deal with the sociological point of view. Even today, many Catholics view the social sciences as territory held by the enemy, and those who have taken the sociological point of view, by and large, have little interest in making sense of traditional Catholic beliefs and practices.

Perhaps some of you are already vexed by my description of Christopher Dawson as a social scientist. In at least two ways, his work did not resemble our image of a social scientist (both have to do with the word *scientist*). In the first place, he was not a number-crunching statistician. He did not practice the kind of sociological "science" found in the corporate and political world. By today's standards, Dawson was closer to being a cultural anthropologist than a sociologist. In the second place, his work was not sequestered to a particular discipline within the university. This is an easy point to make, since Dawson was not a university man. His appointment at Harvard was to the Stillman Chair, not to an ordinary department. If he were to be hired in a university today, he would probably end up in a department of religion.

I use the term *social scientist* in connection with Dawson chiefly in the classical-modern sense of the term—derived from Weber and Durkheim, who worked on the border of such disciplines as history, cultural anthropology, and philosophy. The great pioneers of modern social science were fascinated by the problem of religion and modernity, which was a central issue not only for Weber and Durkheim but also for Freud. Dawson also stood in a slightly older tradition, which I shall call "prophetic sociology", of the sort practiced by Alexis de Tocqueville and perhaps also, in his own way, by Henry Adams. Prophetic sociology is not the same thing as "gadfly sociology", in connection with which Andrew Greeley's name comes to mind. By prophetic sociology, I mean an investigation of social data that leads not so much to scientific generalizations as to a moral or religious vision. Here I am only paraphrasing Dawson's own characterization of Tocqueville, with whom he closely identified.[2]

In his book *The Crisis of Western Education,* Dawson emphasized that the curriculum should reflect the "sociological character" of the subject.[3] There can be no doubt but that, in matters of education, Dawson wished to subordinate the aesthetic-literary, the philosophical, and the theological to the sociological. Notice that I said "subordinate", not "reduce". It would never have entered his mind that the so-called sociological point of view is reductive, for Dawson's understanding of history and culture was eschatological—he remained throughout his life an Augustinian. By "sociological", he meant something very simple, which I think can be described in a sentence or two. One adopts the sociological point of view when he takes institutions, and the processes by which they are built and eventually decay, as a subject for inquiry antecedent to a detailed study of the intellectual and aesthetic artifacts of those institutions. More simply put, and to take one of Dawson's own examples, one should first understand the institution and culture

of monasticism and then turn to monastic philosophy, illumi-
nated manuscripts, and the other artifacts of the institution.

II

In the time remaining, I would like to examine a current issue
which requires, or at least favors, the sociological point of
view — and about which Dawson still has something important to say to us. No doubt, there are other issues that could
be fruitfully discussed in the light of Dawsonian themes. The
one I shall discuss, however, is the issue of the college curriculum, and whether or not we should be interested in a canon
of great books. The recent debates at Stanford, Allan Bloom's
book, and the circumlocutions of our past secretary of education have brought this issue to the forefront of public attention.

In *The Crisis of Western Education,* Dawson wrote: "What we
need is not an encyclopedic knowledge of all the products of
Christian culture, but a study of the culture-process itself from
its spiritual and theological roots, through its organic historical growth to its cultural fruits."[4] As I said earlier, he was interested first in the cultural process of social institutions and
only then in the literary and philosophical achievements of the
institutions. This explains, in part, why he was relatively more
interested in the formative period of Western culture (the so-
called Dark Ages) than the high medieval period.[5] For Dawson,
the primitive or incipient stages are more sociologically interesting than the fully developed flower of a culture. This focus is
entirely understandable to historians and sociologists, but I
should mention in passing that it made it very difficult for the
scholastic establishment in Catholic schools to hear what Dawson was saying on this score some thirty years ago. Scholastic
philosophy abstracts the intellectual geometry from the culture
and, for good reason, is more interested in the highly developed
intellectual systems of the thirteenth century than in the sociology of barbarian peoples north of Italy in the seventh century.

Far be it from me to criticize intellectual abstraction, since it is what I do for a living; and as far as I am concerned, in comparison with the pop psychology and pop sociology in schools today, we could use more rather than less rigorous philosophical training. But there is an important difference between what it means to abstract and what it means to prescind from culture. All intellectual disciplines, including sociology, require abstraction, which is nothing other than generalizing from particulars. It is quite another thing, however, to prescind from culture. *Prescind,* from the Latin, means to "cut off". Since Descartes, philosophers have believed that there is such a thing as noncultural starting points for inquiry; that, by methodological fiat, the inquirer can prescind from culture for the purpose of "seeing" reality more accurately. This, rather than abstraction, is the problem. As the cultural anthropologist Clifford Geertz has remarked, the heritage of the Enlightenment is the image of "man as a naked reasoner [who appears as he truly is only] when he took his cultural costumes off".[6] This not only leads to the distorted idea that there can be a traditionless *body of knowledge,* but it also hides the fact that culture is a second nature, in the womb of which virtually all of our thinking is formed. One can admit that ideas have sociological feet without being a relativist or reductionist. Aristotle, after all, argued that it is our habits (both moral and intellectual), working conjointly with our first nature, which make us in any determinate way what we are.

Long before the term *enculturation* became fashionable, Dawson equated it with *education* in the broadest sense of the term. The purpose of education is to understand how cultures are formed, transmitted, and received by the individual — not just Western culture but non-Western cultures as well.[7] In fact, in the *Crisis of Western Education,* Dawson wrote that it is necessary "to make the student aware of the relativity of culture".[8] Dawson did not believe this was a capitulation to secularism but, rather, the way out of it; for the self-centered world of secular and popular culture presents itself as the only optic on reality. Dawson here had an Augustinian diagnosis of modernity as a kind of spiritual autism.[9] A healthy sense of cultural relativism is needed to break out of that loop. After what we have seen in the school systems these past two decades, one might wonder whether Dawson was out of his mind when he recommended a heightened sense of cultural relativity; but I think he was correct. Students do not really have a sense of cultural relativity but are trapped in the perspective of popular culture, having no more sense of how their grandparents lived than of how people arrange their institutions in Indonesia. The problem is that students are under the impression that one can have all of the goodies of a culture (ranging from material artifacts like VCRs, to more noumenal artifacts like "great ideas", to legal artifacts like a Bill of Rights) without learning how these things, ideas, or legal systems are culturally conditioned and traduced.

In the *Closing of the American Mind* (1987), Allan Bloom had his finger close to the nerve of the issue when he charged that popular culture occludes or clouds the minds of the students. Unfortunately, Bloom's remarks in this vein crossed over into a diatribe against social scientists; in so doing, he flubbed a golden opportunity to point out that students need more rather than less training in what is sociologically specific to the West — or, for that matter, what is specific to any particular culture. It is interesting that, on this same problem of the circumambient influence of popular culture, Dawson looked to the social sciences as a crucial part of the solution. He wrote:

> The position of modern American education is very paradoxical. On the one hand . . . the dominant tendency of American society is towards social conformity, and public education has strengthened this tendency by its uncritical attitude towards "the American Way of Life" and the current democratic ideology. But on the other hand Americans have had exceptional opportunities to understand the diversity of culture, owing not only to the differences of their own cultural origins, but also to the fact that from the beginning of American history they have been

brought into contact with native American peoples who followed
a completely different way of life. It has been the American anthro-
pologists who have led the way in the study of these different ways
of life and who also were, I believe, the first to formulate the concept of *culture* as the fundamental object of scientific social study.[10]

Dawson goes on to recommend the work of Margaret Mead.
Whereas one might suspect that Bloom's answer to popular culture is a Pythagorean summer camp without radios, Dawson
does not recommend more attention to universals but, rather,
to a study of determinate cultures in all of their particularity.

I want briefly to point out why Dawson's understanding of
education cuts against the grain of certain conservative and
progressive theories of education today. In the first place,
Dawson's approach was quite different from a "great books"
program. Indeed, he explicitly rejected the notion that his program of studies was a refined exposure to great literature. While
I am sure that he would not have denied the idea that there
can be a relatively nonarbitrary canon of great books, he also
understood that one can read the artifacts of a culture and still
be ignorant about the culture itself, and what sets it off from
any other culture. I teach Saint Anselm in philosophy classes
every year, but I am not at all convinced that the students have
the slightest notion of the institution of monasticism, the pattern of medieval culture, or what separates it from modernity.
So here I will speak for myself. The notion of a great books
program can be a conservative smorgasbord — a bag of nouns
without the rest of the cultural grammar. And insofar as this
is the case, it reflects the worst of the modern mind, even
though it is usually styled as a conservative alternative to
Deweyanism. John Dewey, we recall, insisted that education
should be practical rather than speculative. True enough, in
contrast to Dewey, a great books course of studies would seem
to reaffirm the traditional primacy given to the contemplative
over the practical. What I mean by the worst of modernity is
the notion that a student can have immediate access to a world

of ideas without having to pass through the cultural media which traduce those ideas; accordingly, the student is relieved of the burden of having to reckon with, to avow, and ultimately to live in one culture rather than another.

A set of ideas or books, without an historical and a cultural context, is neither conservative nor, for that matter, coherent. For example, if one reads the required book list for freshmen at Columbia University (1937–38), one notices nothing between Augustine and Dante. Nearly 800 years are off the map. Now, if one is principally interested in literature, this is perhaps not so surprising. But if one is interested in Western culture, the 800-year gap is devastating; for some of the central aspects of Western culture evolved during that time, including monasticism, universities, and the distinction between ecclesial and secular jurisdictions. (Incidentally, nothing from the Bible is to be found on the list, nor are any of the great treatises of the Reformation, which is just as well, since those treatises would be virtually unintelligible without presupposing a thing or two about the Bible.) If I can be permitted a gratuitous sideswipe at Allan Bloom, the curriculum I am describing here was formulated thirty years before the 1960s. It is ahistorical and traditionless; so perhaps the reaction of the 1960s regarding cultural relevance can be reconsidered in a more favorable light.

The Columbia curriculum of 1937 could be read as reflecting the altogether typical modern effort to censure matters of religion—whether Jewish, Christian, or Islamic. I am not the first person to notice or to point out that most great books programs developed out of the University of Chicago orbit gave little place to matters of religion; and this is not so much a symptom of irreligion as it is a reflection of an Olympian disdain for empirical culture and history. For if one continues to read the Columbia list chronologically, there is likewise nothing to indicate the emergence of the modern state, state-sponsored science, or modern political economy—in short, those sociological realities most distinctive of modernity. The reading list simply does not touch base with history and social institutions.

To summarize, a great books program strikes me as deficient on two scores. On the one hand, it lacks the virtue of pre-modern education, in which the student was a participant in a concrete and determinate way of life. When Thomas More, for example, educated his daughter in the classics, the program was not an ersatz academic culture unrelated to one's familiar institutions but was, rather, a process of appropriating the culture one already avowed. On the other hand, it lacks one of modernity's most interesting self-correctives, which is the heightened awareness of historical contingency and of diverse cultures. The social sciences at least can make one aware that the modern culture is not the only way that human beings have culturally reproduced themselves. This was Dawson's point about the value of sociology. I want to amplify the point, and say that one should not drink from the well of modernity without swallowing the pill of the social sciences. One needs an antidote for that kind of water.

On the other side of the issue, the progressives not only drink the water of modernity, and swallow the pill, but continue to swallow the pill. Since the 1960s, their criticism has moved along one or another of these two lines. First, it is argued that there is no such thing as a traditionless, ahistorical, and decultured hierarchy of knowledge. With some qualifications, this claim is more than a half-truth, which, unfortunately, is usually canceled out by the next line of thought. Second, it is asserted that these hierarchies are nothing but thinly veiled expressions of power, reflecting the imperialism of a gender, class, race, or whatever. Those who follow the first line call for cultural relevance — namely, that ideas and lists of books reflect more closely the cultural grounds. They insist that more works by women, third worlders, blacks, etc., be represented in order to broaden perspective. Those who follow the second line are not satisfied with cultural relevance and diversity but, rather, insist that all claims be unmasked as a will to power. As Michel Foucault argues, educational curricula (like hospitals, prisons, and modern factories) are modern institutions in which the inner life is made public for the purposes of surveillance, discipline, and the exercise of power.[11] Foucault is probably the most influential social theorist of our time; it is his work that is in the background of the Stanford controversy. From what I have been able to gather from it — that is, from reading and from having to teach it — Foucault's work is powerful precisely because he reaches into the historical and empirical level of social institutions, taking liberal pieties about rights and liberation and then examining them on a level that the liberal Brahmins of our educational institutions disdain. Foucault's work is dark; morally, it is a dead end; but I can understand why young faculty and students are enthralled and why they do not believe that Secretary Bennett and Allan Bloom have the foggiest idea of what they are talking about.

The two prongs of the progressive critique (cultural relevance and the will-to-power thesis) often go hand in hand in the academy today. For example, in a recent forum in *Harper's,* Ellen Spivak (an Andrew Mellon Professor of English and Cultural Studies at the University of Pittsburgh) argued on the one hand that the canon of great books must reflect not only the culture of Old Europe but also the history of Africans and Native Americans — giving special emphasis to the history of slavery and genocide of non-Western peoples; on the other hand, she contended that the legacy of Western humanism is "the story of the straight, white, Christian man of property" — a story that "covers up" other stories and therefore is an "unacknowledged power play".[12] Every document of culture, she warns, is a document of barbarism.

There are many problems with this self-engulfing sociology. *First,* one begins by asserting the primacy of the sociological approach to ideas, which in turn yields the position that culture is not valuable; indeed, the sociological approach itself is only another instance of will to power. There is nothing in principle to prevent the judgment that these young professors are using Foucault to make their own professional power play. *Second,* historically speaking, it is amazing that anyone should claim

that the story of Western humanism is the story of white, hetero-
sexual men of property: (a) Homer, Aristotle, Augustine, and
the authors of the Scriptures were not "white" men; Socrates
and Plato were perhaps not entirely "straight". (b) Virtually
none of the medieval works were written by men of property.
Spivak's remark in this regard indicates, despite herself, the need
to ground great books in history and culture: she does not seem
to recognize the most elementary facts about the racial and cultural pluralism of the Mediterranean peoples. The conservative response is that ideas transcend race and gender, but my
point is rather that one first needs to see them in their particular cultural and sociological settings. (c) Although the canon
overwhelmingly includes male authors, the notion that those
who write books are the most powerful and prestigious members of the culture is a rather Western assumption. *Third,* the
suggestion that we should, as Dawson once complained,[13] kick
away the ladder of European historiography would be in vain,
for Spivak's own claims make sense only from a Eurocentric
perspective. The imperialism that she decries makes sense, of
course, only against the backdrop of European colonialism and
the international scope of that expansion. Any effort to understand non-European cultures (such as Indochina) without understanding the ideologies spawned in Europe and implanted
internationally is doomed—much of Asia lives under regimes
organized by a nineteenth-century German ideology. In this
regard, I am reminded of a theology professor I had as an undergraduate, who recommended that the class read *Black Elk
Speaks.* The book, he opined, showed that Sioux Indians had
a well-developed theological culture that was in many ways
"Christian", perhaps more Christian than conventional Christianity. Several years later, quite by accident, I learned that Black
Elk was a Jesuit-trained catechist. So much for ideas and books
that fail to connect with actual historical conditions.

Finally, the progressive position does not really draw the
mind to cultural pluralism but, rather, constitutes an ersatz, syn-
cretic culture having reality only in the minds of academicians.

If the conservative great books programs are a bag of nouns, the progressive versions are a bag of verbs, reflecting reactions against Western culture by literate academicians. For example, if we look at the list of books recommended for the course "Culture, Ideas, Values" last year at Stanford, one *does* find Augustine, Freud, the Bible, Weber, and Shakespeare; but one also finds texts with titles like these: *Black Jacobins; Voodoo in Haiti; In Defense of the Indians; Vindication of the Rights of Women; The Woman Warrior; Travel in Hyperreality*. I am probably revealing my ignorance, but I have never heard of at least a third of the books on the list. For all I know, they are good books. But my point is that the list does not reflect any concrete culture or any culture-forming process. One doubts that the book *Voodoo in Haiti* represents an interest in Caribbean culture.

The progressives at Stanford and elsewhere, despite themselves, are providing a service. One can, with certain qualifications, be sympathetic to their critique; for what they have done is to call the bluff on what remains of Western humanism. The bluff is this: that one can enjoy the artifacts of a culture without enculturation in the process that produces those artifacts: (1) that one can grasp at even an elementary level what is going on in Augustine's *Confessions* without knowing something about the difference between Christian prayer and psychoanalytic introspection; (2) that one can grasp the ideas in the Declaration of Independence without any appreciation for the religious and cultural context; (3) that one can recommend Shakespeare's sonnets to students even while recommending in the real culture the primacy of television — as in the 1960s, when authorities tacitly admitted the equality if not the supremacy of pop culture while trying to hold the line on the curriculum. There is no such thing as traditionless knowledge, no art or ideational products outside of institutions, no culture without religion. It seems to me that the progressives have called this bluff. Why should one read the *Song of Roland* rather than *The Woman Warrior* or Augustine's *Confessions* rather than *Voodoo in Haiti*? Judgments of this sort cannot prescind from cul-

ture; even if a book has transcultural meaning and value, one
cannot start there; the judgment moves from the particular to
the universal. Failing to stand in a cultural tradition, claims
about the relative superiority of certain ideas or books will appear to be just what the radicals say they are—namely, asser-
tions of power. Like recommending that people learn English
or a computer language, one might argue that the more tradi-
tional-looking canons of great books have value because they
are practical—which is another way of saying that they help
people accommodate themselves to a power structure. I am not
sure that the liberal Brahmins of our schools have any argument left.

III

Dawson's theory of education will go nowhere today. First,
it focuses upon Christian culture as being the specific backbone
of the West. Second, it defends the Eurocentric perspective—
which is one of the main points of his book *Christianity in East
and West.* Any effort today even to suggest that one needs the
Western perspective if only to understand the plight of the non-
Western world is doomed to failure. Third, the modern university is too bureaucratically complicated to enact any curricular
reform as nuanced as Dawson's. If you go back and look at
his program in *The Crisis of Western Education,* you will see that
he wanted to organize the curriculum according to an historical scheme: the student is introduced to subjects like law and
art and philosophy as the subject matter emerged from within
particular cultures. History departments cannot organize history that way, and it is entirely unrealistic to expect a univer-
sity-wide curriculum of this sort. Nevertheless, the general
point Dawson wanted to make about the importance of history and sociology is still valid. What is important today are
not the details of Dawson's curriculum but the problem it was
geared to address.

Dawson's ideas were by and large rejected by Catholic educators. The program was viewed either as insufficiently scholastic or as too interdisciplinary for the modern university. But the same people who regarded Dawson suspiciously then were the ones who presided over the dismantling of scholastic philosophy and theology a few years later. About the time of Dawson's death, Catholic educators in America declared the older forms of knowledge to be provincial, obsolete, and foisted upon Catholics by ecclesiastical authority. The whole thing was acted out just as Dawson predicted it would be.[14] To argue that students ought to have three courses in philosophy is to draw upon an historical context of shared expectations about how various disciplines and inquiries ought to be integrated; to argue that all students must have courses in human nature, metaphysics, and ethics is to presuppose somewhat more; and to suppose that the content of those courses should give a prominent place to Aquinas' philosophy is to assume an even more specific history. As a general rule of thumb, I believe it is true to say that the material that has the most transcendent and transcultural value is also the material that rests most precariously upon contingent and historical sensibilities, requiring the kind of training that only a determinate cultural tradition can afford. When the cultural tradition is lost, it becomes virtually impossible to argue for the value of its artifacts.

Alasdair MacIntyre has recently (1988) written a book entitled *Whose Justice? Which Rationality?* One of the main points of the book is that moral and legal conceptions of justice are rooted in traditions and institutions. MacIntyre points out that discourse about justice becomes fruitless if none of the interlocutors are themselves rooted in a tradition. Discussion and inquiry into the relative merit and superiority of ideas must begin somewhere. What we have seen in the Stanford debate is the fruitlessness of starting from nowhere — by which I mean that none of the parties to the dispute are willing to live in and avow the historical and cultural contexts of the ideas or lists of ideas. Rather, as I said, the context turns out to be an ersatz academic culture, unrelated in any concrete way to a real culture (either past or present, either mainline or marginal). And this is what Catholic schools are coming to resemble; for, as anyone who teaches in a Catholic school can attest, what is billed as the uniquely Catholic component of the college (campus ministry) usually turns out to be a weird little subculture, like the bar in *Star Wars*, that has little connection to any sociological reality beyond the gates of the campus. This, I suggest, is precisely what Dawson feared and tried to warn his American audience about some thirty years ago. The problem cuts deeper than issues of orthodoxy and heterodoxy, for those issues already presuppose some determinate sense of history and culture.

The Catholic Intellectual Renaissance earlier in this century made extraordinary contributions in literature, philosophy, and theology. It did not happen by accident. Catholic institutions, as well as the surrounding secular culture of the late nineteenth century, still contained the conditions for a renewal of those disciplines. Today, any prospect for another renaissance of Catholic thought will require a more direct reckoning with the social sciences—both for their diagnostic power and for the reminder that all of the important things have sociological feet.

NOTES

[1] James Hitchcock, "Postmortem on a Rebirth: The Catholic Intellectual Renaissance", *American Scholar,* Spring 1980, p. 108.

[2] Christopher Dawson, "The Problem of Metahistory", in *Dynamics of World History,* ed. John Mulloy (Lasalle, Ill.: Sherwood Sugden & Co., 1978), p. 293.

[3] Christopher Dawson, *The Crisis of Western Education* (New York: Sheed & Ward, 1961), p. 155.

[4] Ibid., p. 137.

[5] See my discussion of this point in "The Metahistorical Vision of Christopher Dawson", in *The Dynamic Character of Christian Culture,* ed. Peter Cataldo (Lanham, Md.: University Press of America, 1984).

[6] Clifford Geertz, "The Impact of the Concept of Culture on the Concept of Man", in *The Interpretation of Cultures* (New York: Basic Books, 1973), p. 35.

[7] Dawson, *Crisis,* p. 3.

[8] Ibid., p. 147.

[9] Ibid., p. 178.

[10] Ibid., p. 147.

[11] Michel Foucault, *Discipline and Punish: The Birth of the Prison,* trans. Alan Sheridan (New York: Vintage Books, 1979).

[12] "Who Needs the Great Works?" *Harper's,* Sept. 1989, p. 47.

[13] See my essay referred to in note 5 above, pp. 44ff.

[14] Dawson, *Crisis,* p. 150.

EDWARD A. SYNAN

GILSON REMEMBERED

One need not be a Scotist of the strict observance to concede that John Duns Scotus was right to have written: "Negationes etiam non summe amamus" (Negations, to be sure, are not what we prize most highly).[1] Still, with all respect to the shades of the Subtle Doctor, as Scotus was understandably dubbed, my opening guns on "Gilson Remembered" must be two negations.

First, to attempt a biography of Étienne Gilson does not seem to be appropriate. Apart from the daunting character of a project that would compress almost ninety-five years into an oral summary of tolerable length, the thing has been done, and done with consummate skill. L. K. Shook, C.S.B., had the cooperation of Gilson himself in putting together the more than 400 pages that constitute *Étienne Gilson: A Biography*.[2]

Second, there was in the early 1950s a most distressing international misunderstanding, briefly called the "Gilson affair on neutralism"; it arose from an article by a professor of political philosophy in December of 1950; it ended only in October of 1951, when the author of the offending article wrote his apologies to Gilson: "I ought to have cited in a public discussion only your public expressions of your views. In citing from private conversations I was at fault and beg your pardon."[3]

This whole matter is better forgotten—except as a cautionary instance of what not to do. The memories you will hear are, therefore, either of what Gilson said in public (even if in the restricted "public" of lecture hall or seminar room) or of what one can be sure he would not have objected to our recalling here, even though it was pronounced in private conversation. A scholastic (which Gilson most definitely was not!)

would say that "material" privacy need not be taken to coincide with "formal" privacy at all points. In fact, only one conversation comes to mind as not to be cited. In it, Gilson expressed a strong and pejorative view of a most eminent public figure. To my certain knowledge, he modified this view dramatically a year or two later. Despite a certain temptation to do so, it is a point of honor to report neither the great name nor Gilson's witty condemnation, pronounced as it was before a small company of colleagues and soon reversed. Gilson himself once wrote that the Lord "*knows* essences" (that is, the Creator knows all that can possibly be), "but He *says* existences, and He does not say all that He knows."[4] In our diminished way, so it must be with us: we ought not to say all that we happen to know.

If you will not hear all I know about Gilson, owing to constraints of time and prudence, neither will you hear what I do not know about him. You have my promise not to go beyond facts that are known to me to be facts. In this, my aim is to blunt the edge of the axe that Aristotle honed against those multitudinous masters of anecdote (The Philosopher said "all", and surely there are many) who stretch the truth in order to "entertain". "We all tell a story with additions — and think by this to do our hearers a pleasure."[5] May you agree that Gilson's story needs no additions!

In any event, my remarks must be anecdotal and impressionistic, rather than systematic. If they carry an inevitable tinge of autobiography, your consolation must be that, if this is a heavy price to pay for an eyewitness account, it is also a warranty of its truth.

You will have inferred from this that my direct experience of the man himself will be a major resource in these remarks; and so, it may be feared, biography having been renounced, autobiography is threatened.

Now it is a graceless thing to submit kind hosts to uncovenanted autobiography. On the other hand, only a few former students of Étienne Gilson, all of us old now, have had with him the contacts, direct and indirect, comparable to those which have enriched my life. During four years, it was my happy lot to be one of his students at the Pontifical Institute of Mediaeval Studies in Toronto. After a seven-year stint of teaching at Seton Hall, there were fourteen years during which Gilson and I were colleagues on the staff of the institute in Toronto. During the last of those years, I was its president. When Gilson died in 1978, I was present — along with his biographer and former president of the institute, L. K. Shook — at his funeral in the Cathedral of Saint Stephen in Auxerre. At his graveside in Melun (a town in which Peter Abelard had conducted a school), Shook and I heard the words of the incomparable M. D. Chenu, O.P., as the body of our old friend was buried beside that of his wife. Of his wife, Thérèse, when she died during my second year at the institute, Gilson had been able to say: "No one before, no one during, no one after."

All of this came to pass long after I had come to know Gilson. As was the case with most during Gilson's lifetime, and since his death with all, my contact with Gilson was first through his writing.

One sunny spring evening in 1937, a monk with whom I was friendly, Hugh Duffy, O.S.B., met me walking down the main driveway of the Seton Hall College campus, where my third undergraduate year was coming to its end. Duffy asked me where he might find the president of the college. At that moment, we had a new and picturesque president at Seton Hall, James F. Kelley, who rejoiced in a new doctorate in philosophy from Louvain and a reputation to match. Hugh Duffy and I went to the president's office, where the appropriate introductions were made. Before discreetly leaving my elders, I was able to read (discreetly also) the title and the author's name on the spine of a book that rested on the otherwise empty expanse of the president's desk. That book was Étienne Gilson's *Spirit of Mediaeval Philosophy,* the English translation of his 1931–32 Gifford Lectures at the University of Aberdeen.[6] In total ignorance of the author, but on the chance that a book on our new president's desk might well be worth reading, I asked my parents to give me a copy. They did so, and on the 15th of December eleven years later Gilson was to autograph that copy for me; of course, I have it still. After more than fifty years, my impression of this first indirect contact with Gilson is still vivid.

Our class at Seton Hall was completing a compulsory first year of philosophy, and, as was usual in those days, the teaching of philosophy was a mixed bag of the good and the bad. The worst of the bad was that Catholic schools seem generally to have taught philosophy through manuals, often (as at Seton Hall) through a manual written in Latin. Ours was the work of an Irish Cistercian named J. S. Hickey, and his three volumes carried the forthright title *Summula philosophiae scholast- sticae* (A brief summary of scholastic philosophy). There was a subtitle as well, which we counted somewhat demeaning and which hardly requires translation: *In usum adolescentium* (for the use of adolescents). The content of the Hickey volumes, as some of us would much later come to realize, was primarily the doctrine of Francisco Suárez, S.J., but not without occasional echoes of the problematic of Descartes.

What was good about using Hickey was that students learned something of a simplified scholastic logic, something about discriminating between the areas of philosophy: between the problems of knowledge and the problems of what ought to be the case, a first acquaintance with traditional analyses of material things, and even a modest grasp of classical definitions and divisions — in short, the panoply and the atmosphere of philosophical discourse in the scholastic manner. Of course, we did not like the book, and it was heartening to find out later that Gilson did not like it either: he has two unfavorable references to our author in his *Réalisme thomiste et critique de la connaissance.*[7]

What was much better for our philosophical training was officially not philosophy at all, but then counted as part of an arts degree program at Seton Hall. In Greek class, we read some Plato, certainly the *Apology,* perhaps also (for memory here is somewhat vague) one or another of the prison dialogues, the

Crito it may have been, or the *Phaedo*. In our sophomore Latin class, a bright new Ph.D. from the Catholic University of America had taken us through a cut-down edition of Saint Augustine's *Confessions*. Thus, we had a limited, but precious, acquaintance with two literary artists, Plato and Augustine, who had been blessed with first-class philosophical minds, supplemented by Hickey's more technical, and not at all literary, manual, suitable for "adolescents".

Against this background, Gilson's *Spirit of Mediaeval Philosophy* burst with the aura of revelation. This, it seemed to me as a nineteen-year-old candidate for the seminary, is what philosophy ought to be: lucid, erudite, literate, grounded in the historically acquired experience of towering human intellects and interpreted, even advanced, by another such intellect of our own time. The first year of our class in the major seminary at Darlington was, academically, our senior year at Seton Hall; philosophically, it was one more year of Hickey. This was not good, but Gilson had shown not only that it could be better but also how it could be better.

When the war had ended and even those with as few points as I had garnered—no combat, no dependents, no personal decorations—drifted back into civilian life, my archbishop sent for me. Time, he said, that I return to Louvain. My first year and a half of theology had been done there at the Collège Américain, but with the understanding that I try later for a doctorate in philosophy. Contrary to what "everybody knows" about archiepiscopal tyranny, Archbishop Walsh customarily told both laymen and clerics what he had in mind, but then would ask: "What do you think of that?" My answer that day was that, although I had loved Louvain, Toronto would be better. "Why?" Because Gilson and Maritain taught there. It did not seem necessary to mention that the direct realism of those two (proposed, to be sure, in their diverse and highly personal ways) seemed right as against the "illative" and "critical" realism then current in the Louvain of Monsignor Noël and that it was Gilson who had persuaded me of this. How far from

the Leuven of today is that old solution and the controversies
it fueled!

Classes opened in early October in 1948. A seminary professor from our seminary at Darlington, whose doctoral work had
been delayed by the war and beyond, was with me there to
begin the three-year license course at the Pontifical Institute
and (as then was possible) to count them against the University of Toronto four-year program for the Ph.D. — provided
that we add some modern philosophy to the Greek and medieval philosophy we would take at the institute.

We were eager to see and to hear Gilson. My first sight of
him was often repeated. He would walk between classes or before lectures beside the gray stone of the institute wing provided
in a building of Saint Michael's College. That first sight of him
was on a bright fall day, brisk but with bright sunlight. He
was with an institute colleague of his, and the sight would be
repeated time without number in the future. Gilson was of
medium height and heavily built; his face was plump, apple-
cheeked, chin pointed and, at that point in his life and to the
end, emphasized by a small, clipped moustache. His hair was
black, and, although it was thinning, he was never to lose it.
A fairly heavy smoker, Gilson usually cupped his cigarette in
the European way; thus was he smoking when first we two
Newark priests saw him.

There is always some diminution of awe when we see our
first cardinal or general or author; the common humanity we
had unconsciously inflated is suddenly before us as one of us;
Gilson, or the pope, is human as we are.

This diminution of awe at the first sight of Gilson was to
be reversed as soon as we heard him from the podium. Before
that, we had been given the normal, and unreliable, indoctrination provided by students from the upper years. Anecdotes
that lost nothing in the telling (as Aristotle had claimed would
be the case) had for their major theme the fast pace set by Gilson in his courses, but especially in his seminars. There was
an ominous undercurrent to suggest that with the fast pace went

a temper on a short leash; and, to tell the truth, this was not altogether without foundation. True enough, none of us ever saw the lightnings flash, but there was a system designed to ground them out. No one signed spontaneously for his seminars; a student was invited to do so by the secretary of the institute. In our time, this office was held by George B. Flahiff, C.S.B.; and, although his post was and is named "secretary", he did what registrars usually do. The trick was not to let questionable students irritate Gilson, and no doubt it had been contrived owing to embarrassing past episodes. It was one thing to be one of hundreds in public lecture courses; it was quite another to be one of seven or ten, seated around a table, exchanging pleasantries on medieval thought with the greatest living master of the field. For he treated us as equals without condescension, but we never could forget that he was first among equals, *primus inter pares.*

Seminars were not the only sessions in which the more personal side of Gilson reached us. In those days, it was customary on Friday afternoons to hold a fairly formal and elaborate tea at the institute for staff, students, and guests, these last often scholars of reputation who were passing through Toronto. Gilson took part whenever he was in the city. Without precisely talking shop, he and we spoke lightly, but with a degree of seriousness, on matters of interest; and this was the locale at which a myth was shattered.

The myth was that Maritain and Gilson fought bitterly over philosophy and over students' dissertations. Because they did have their personal approaches, by no means identical, there was a surface plausibility to such tales; it did not survive the first time I saw and heard them together. Maritain in those years was at the Institute for Advanced Study at Princeton, no longer teaching regularly in Toronto; indeed, when he did teach us, it would be for a tight two or three weeks only, for no credit, on a theme he expected the students to have read up on before he arrived. Naturally, he would come to tea and, as naturally, he and Gilson would meet there. Not only were they evidently on the best of terms, but each was visibly interested in, and respectful of, the straight philosophical views of the other. If they differed, it was with a mutual friendship and understanding; their differences arose from their diverse angles of approach. Both, for instance, were deeply persuaded of the human value of what is now called "fine art", and each was invited to give the A. W. Mellon Lectures at the National Gallery in Washington, D.C. Their two courses are available in two splendid books; those volumes are far from the same.[8] Is art a matter of knowledge? Is art not a knowledge but a making — even, in its fashion, a creation?

One commment by Gilson will serve to put in perspective the gulf that separated these two friends and collaborators on Christian wisdom. When, at the end of his life, the delicate and even mystical Maritain joined the Little Brothers of Jesus, Gilson, in my presence, said of this with wit, affection, and deep respect: "This is something to be admired, not imitated!" It is all there: the robust, commonsensical, down-to-earth Gilson; the ethereal, sensitive, contemplative Maritain. Those of us who have loved them both have no desire to judge between them, to take one over the other. Decades before, as Shook has established and documented in his biography of Gilson, the slightly younger Gilson writing home from the front in 1915 to ask for summaries of Maritain's lecturing had even then long been an admirer of Maritain's thought.

All of us are likely to have heard from older students that our teachers, ogres in the past, have providentially mellowed before we faced them, and something of this attached to the tales of Gilson floating around the Pontifical Institute in those years. One spring, he was in the city at the time of examinations and announced that he would sit on the orals board for a course I had taken with Daniel Callus, O.P., on the Dominicans at Oxford in the early thirteenth century. When it was my turn to face the board, it was Gilson's turn to pose a question and he proceeded to do so on Franciscans at Paris. Neither of the other two examiners (Callus was one) came to my rescue. Gilson pressed me on Roger Bacon and especially on that worthy *Opus maius*. Every seminarian's trick of talking around areas of ignorance failed to deter Gilson: "I stick by my guns", he announced. When I conceded that I had not read the *Opus maius,* he said "Many people have not read it!" and let me go. Perhaps after I left them, the two silent examiners took up my defense; in any case, they gave me ten full marks, and perhaps Gilson went along because he thought I could defend an indefensible position.

If it were necessary to isolate Gilson's best side in his dealing with students, one could not avoid pointing to his concern to let us be ourselves. He was rigorous in requiring that we respect our texts, the methods of the various sciences involved in establishing them and in interpreting their content, but he did not dictate beyond that on what we might make of them. When the late Professor Charles J. O'Neil, himself a former student of Gilson's, edited a volume of studies by a number of his North American students to honor Gilson's thirtieth year as director of studies in the Pontifical Institute, he adverted to the independence of those students:

> Philosophers sometimes have produced only commentator-disciples. . . . When there was question of grouping these studies topically the only thing the editor, Board, and authors could be brought to agree on was the alphabet. Clearly Gilson has the honor of having contributed to the formation of independent scholars.[9]

This generous accolade is not universally granted. Here and there, the term *Gilsonian school* is encountered, at times with a name or two, most often those of Joseph Owens, C.Ss.R., and Armand Maurer, C.S.B. These two were challenged persistently by an unfortunate scholar to reply, not with articles but with a book, to his dissenting views on Thomistic efforts to demonstrate rationally that there is a God. The anti-"Gilsonian school" objector was concerned with the "five ways", but there is another discussion of Divine Being by Brother

Thomas that demonstrates how illusory is the notion that
Owens and Maurer constitute such a school. A passage from
On Being and Essence, written by the young, but already ex-
pert, Aquinas, claims that essence and existence are not identical in creatures, whereas for the Creator, "to be" is "essential".
Is this chapter's argument a "sixth way" to prove that the Divine must be Real?[10] Armand Maurer argues that it is not;
Joseph Owens claims that it is. And Gilson himself? "Contrary
to what we ourselves have once believed, this development is
not intended by Thomas Aquinas to be a proof of the existence of God."[11] And Gilson supports this view with reasons.
At the heart of Thomistic metaphysics, the "study of being as
being" is, of course, "Being Itself" — for theologians and for simple believers, the God of Exodus 3:14. If this is true, then the
"Gilsonian school" on this point consists of one disciple who
holds what Gilson at one point did not yet see and another disciple who still holds what Gilson had ceased to hold. Which
evaluation is correct: that of the critic who wanted a response
on demonstrations of Divine Being from the two leading
representatives of the "Gilsonian school" or that of the editor
who thought Gilson's students so hopelessly independent as
to require the alphabetical listing of their twenty names — the
only way to reduce their diversity to an intelligible order?

It will surprise no one who knows how enormous the literary legacy of Gilson is that with him the beginning of the written word was often the spoken word.[12] He was first and last
a teacher. His normal practice was to present a lecture course
or seminar, and a year or two later that material would be a
book. In preparing these reminiscences, I have been able to
verify this procedure of his from a lecture course and a seminar on Duns Scotus, the notes of which I still possess. One
notebook contains a seminar that Gilson began with us the fall
his wife sickened and died; Gilson went back to France as soon
as word of her worsening condition reached him, and A.C.
Pegis took over the seminar on the Seventh Quodlibet of Duns
Scotus: Whether it can be demonstrated by natural and neces-

sary reasons that God is omnipotent? The materials in my notebook can be matched on pages 355–75 of Gilson's 1952 mono-
graph on the Subtle Doctor, *Jean Duns Scot: Introduction à ses
positions fondamentales.*[13] The seminar took place in the fall of
1949. The next year, we followed a lecture course on the human soul, which ended with some final reflections on what is
not soul but matter. These issues are found in the same mono-
graph, pages 478–624 on the soul, pages 432–44 on matter. These
notes I took in 1950. As he said to some of us one day, "It is
easy to write a book; all you need is two piles of paper, one
pile for your text, one pile for the notes." He might have added
that it helps to have given a course in the subject of the book.

All of this puts no strain on the credulity of anyone who has
read even one book by Gilson. Another side can be perceived
in his "It is easy to write a book." His wit was quick, tren-
chant, often biting. He was a worthy subject for the ancient
literary form known as doxography, collections of sayings
ascribed to the philosophers and scholars of Greek antiquity.
Nothing was so likely to rouse his sometimes harsh response
as what he took to be pompous or trivial or pretentious. Instances that come to mind often enough bore on academics;
someone professed to admire the eagerness of our students to
begin their careers in research and teaching. Gilson countered:
"Yes; it is easier than working in a factory." On another occasion, a comparable pronouncement led him to say: "To be a
professor is wonderful; all your personal mistakes become
official doctrine."

In another mood, he could provide a line that revealed a simplicity of soul, combined with his enormous erudition. Although
it is briefly recounted by Shook (page 76), a story he told us
one day in a seminar to make some point—a point now forgotten by me at least—had to do with his helping a dying soldier at the front, who, in his delirium, mistook Gilson for the
chaplain and wanted to confess his sins. "I remembered", Gilson told us, "that Albert the Great had said that, in the absence
of a priest, a layman can hear a confession. So I heard his con-

fession, he died consoled, and I have never told anyone what I heard!" Faithful to Gilson's stricture against leaving a point unchecked, I went directly from the seminar to the *Opera omnia* of Albert; there under the heading "On Penance" was Albert's solution: a priest reconciles us with the Lord, but any layman can reconcile us with the Church of God, and so, in the absence of a priest, it is legitimate to confess to a layman.[14] Can we think there was any other young officer in the French (or any other) army who knew what Albert had to say on the point? Must we not think that for the poor dying *poilu,* Gilson was a uniquely providential grace?

This anecdote is a suitable note on which to say something of Gilson's attitude toward priests. Contrary to a general conviction, priests as students in the Pontifical Institute, in my time at least, have been rare. On staff, however, although not proportionately so numerous now as in the past, there is a fair cadre. In any event, from the beginning, Gilson dealt with priests in Toronto. Henry Carr, C.S.B., was with him cofounder of the institute and its first president; Gerald B. Phelan, a diocesan from Halifax, was its first librarian and second president. Gilson, from the foundation until his retirement in his eighties, was director of studies. Toward priests he manifested two attitudes in two situations. On the academic, the scientific, the research side, he was blind to holy orders. Apart from that specialized circumstance, he dealt with priests with unfailing courtesy and respect. On one occasion, it seemed to me that his respect for me was excessive. An American priest had sent him a copy of a book the priest had written on a theological issue. Gilson told me about the book and then gave it to me; this book, he said, "is suitable only for a theologian; it is better that you have it". One day, in return for this courtesy, it seemed right to give Gilson a copy of a book I had written on one aspect of medieval Jewish experience. "Those people!" he said, "I owe them everything!" No doubt, he was thinking especially of Lévy-Bruhl and Bergson, but I could not help remembering that Gilson was ten years old when Captain

Dreyfus was court-martialed and sent to Devil's Island; he was a young man when Dreyfus was finally reinstated. Very late in his time at Toronto, around 1970, when he was quartered next door to my room, one Sunday morning turned out to be a morning of ice that had fallen on snow. Gilson was by then fearful of falling and, because his legs were beginning to give out, was becoming heavier and heavier through lack of exercise. I knocked on his door and told him how icy the paths were and suggested that he come to a small chapel in the same building, where I could offer Mass for him. He accepted as would a child who has been unexpectedly released from a fearsome danger; the two of us alone offered in our diverse fashion the sacrifice by which we both lived. When mass was over, I helped him to the dining room in another building over paths from which most of the ice had melted, and he accepted the help with a childlike simplicity, just as he had accepted my offer of mass in his own building.

If you will not object to this train of associations, there was yet another occasion on which he, deliberately this time, played the child. It was an evening of readings from the poetry of Paul Claudel that he gave to the Toronto Cercle Français in an auditorium on campus. One of the poems represents a child, tired at the end of the day, collapsing unwillingly into sleep. Gilson imitated *ad unguem* the drowsy child's gradual loss of clarity in his speech and the way in which a small child stretches as fatigue conquers a small frame.

The significance of all this is the combination in this great scholar of the most sophisticated erudition with disarming simplicity. In more serious circumstances, this characteristic meant that he could transcend, where appropriate, the control of the academic that so easily becomes tyrannical. You will perhaps not have forgotten that our old manual of philosophy in use at Seton Hall so long ago was described as heavily Suárezian and also that Gilson had made pejorative comments on the manual. Needless to say, perhaps, Gilson did not follow Suárez in his philosophical and theological positions. We all knew this; yet one day in a lecture he mentioned that he had stumbled on some devotional writing by Francisco Suárez. "This", said Gilson, "is the real Suárez: not the *Disputationes metaphysicae*." What was the work that so took Gilson's imagination? Alas, I no longer remember; perhaps it was the great Jesuit's *De mysteriis vitae Christi*. In any event, it helped me in a comparable disenchantment with a more modern theologian whose speculative positions do not seem defensible to me. One day, I saw a work of his on the spiritual life advertised and, remembering Gilson on Suárez, ordered a copy. My reaction was the same; on the life of the spirit, on prayer, on the love of God and neighbor, the author whose speculations seem so unjustifiable came through as a reliable guide where the last goal of the theologian lies in wait for us all.

Still in the current of free association, a last characteristic of Gilson as a lecturer comes to mind with admonitory force. He never went over his allotted time. As he approached the end of that span, he would turn over pages unread: they had been craftily organized to allow a smooth ending. After hearing so much of his long lifetime of writing and of lecturing, of respecting priests, and of letting students find their own voices, may one last tribute to his memory be observed? Having shared with you the reminiscences of one of the least of his students, it seems right to imitate his regard for those who listened and to grant you the boon of silence.

NOTES

[1] *Doctoris subtilis et Mariani Ioannis Duns Scoti, Opera omnia* (Vatican City: Tipographia Poliglotta Vaticana, 1954), *Ordinatio in 1 Sent.*, d. 3, pars 1, qq. 1, 2, tome 3, p. 5, 1.1.

[2] L. K. Shook, C.S.B., *Étienne Gilson: A Biography* (Toronto: Pontifical Institute of Mediaeval Studies, 1984).

[3] Ibid., p. 309.

[4] Étienne Gilson, *Being and Some Philosophers* (Toronto: Pontifical Institute of Mediaeval Studies, 1949), p. 177.

[5] Aristotle, *Poetics* 24.1460a17–19.

[6] Étienne Gilson, *The Spirit of Mediaeval Philosophy* (Gifford Lectures 1931–32), trans. A. H. C. Downes (New York: Scribner's, 1936).

[7] Étienne Gilson, *Réalisme thomiste et critique de la connaissance* (Paris: J. Vrin, 1947); reference to Hickey's *Summulae*, p. 32, n. 1 and p. 33, n. 1.

[8] Jacques Maritain, *Creative Intuition in Art and Poetry*, the A. W. Mellon Lectures in the Fine Arts (New York: Pantheon Books, 1953); reprinted in French, but without illustrations, in *Jacques et Raïssa Maritain: Oeuvres complètes* (Fribourg and Paris: Éditions Saint Paul, 1985), tome 10, pp. 101–601; Étienne Gilson, *Painting and Reality*, the A. W. Mellon Lectures in the Fine Arts (New York: Meridian Books, 1959).

[9] *An Étienne Gilson Tribute*, ed. C. J. O'Neil (Milwaukee: Marquette University Press, 1959), p. vi.

[10] *St. Thomas Aquinas: On Being and Essence*, 2d ed., trans. (with introduction and notes) Armand Maurer, C.S.B. (Toronto: Pontifical Institute of Mediaeval Studies, 1968), pp. 25–26.

[11] Étienne Gilson, *The Christian Philosophy of St. Thomas Aquinas*, trans. L. K. Shook, C.S.B. (New York: Random House, 1956), p. 82.

[12] Margaret McGrath, *Étienne Gilson: A Bibliography/Une bibliographie* (Toronto: Pontifical Institute of Mediaeval Studies, 1982), pp. 124; 1,210 items (15 non-printed materials).

[13] Étienne Gilson, *Jean Duns Scot: Introduction à ses positions fondamentales* (Paris: J. Vrin, 1952).

[14] Albert the Great, *In 4 Sent.*, d. 17, a. 39.

MICHAEL NOVAK

A SALUTE TO JACQUES MARITAIN

Although the twentieth century was often proclaimed by the
Church to be the "Age of the Laity", it remains true that most
Catholic discourse is still taken up with the words, often bril-
liant, of popes, bishops, priests, and sisters. Nonetheless, as in
the nineteenth century so in the twentieth, a number of laymen and women have appeared in the firmament of intellect
and the arts to place the entire body of Christians in their debt.
Of these, no one has been more influential in different spheres
than Jacques Maritain, who is also most widely loved (and es-
teemed for his holiness of life). I do not think that anyone has
written more beautifully of, to cite his title, *Creative Intuition
in Art and Poetry* — perhaps ever, down the ages, in any tradition. (So lovely is that book that often, while reading it as a
undergraduate, I had to put the pages down and go for a long
walk, my heart burning with more than it could bear.)

In political and social thought, no Christian has ever written a more profound defense of the democratic idea and its component parts, such as the dignity of the person; the sharp
distinction between society and the state; the role of practical
wisdom; the common good; the transcendent anchoring of
human rights; transcendent judgment upon societies; and the
interplay of goodness and evil in human individuals and institutions. Indeed, in the thrust that this body of thought gave
to Christian Democratic parties after World War II, Maritain
gained the right to be thought of as one of the architects of
Christian Democracy both in Europe and Latin America.

Nonetheless, it is perhaps in his profound grasp of the metaphysics of the *philosophia perennis* that one must seek the roots

of Maritain's achievement. More clearly and subtly than anyone else in modern times, and over a larger body of materials,
Maritain grasped the "intuition of being" that animates the
deepest stratum of Catholic intellectual life. For him, this was
at once an intuition of charity as well as of being. He chose
most often to express this intuition philosophically — philosophy, not theology, was his vocation; but his vision of *caritas,*
"the Love that moves the sun and all the stars", broke through
in a great many places (not least in his beautiful essays com-
paring Saint Augustine and Saint Thomas, situating the work
of Saint John of the Cross, and describing "knowledge by con-
naturality").

A number of writers, indeed, have pointed out that of all
Maritain's books no doubt the most seminal, like a pebble
plunked in a quiet pool and rippling outward in expanding con-
centric circles, is his tiny *Existence and the Existent.* This "Essay
on Christian Existentialism", a difficult and dense but immensely
pregnant book, lies at the heart of his work. Its brief 142 pages
were penned in Rome from January through April of 1947, as
much of Europe still lay in the ruins of war and as the terribly
disappointing Cold War of the subsequent era was just beginning. Its five compact chapters, I predict, will echo in the
world's thinking for generations to come. Indeed, their full
meaning is likely to become more apparent in the future than
it was at the time of the book's first appearance, particularly
as thinkers from other world traditions make fertile contact
with it.

I would not like it to appear that I see no faults or limits in
Maritain's achievement. Concerned as much as he was for the
poor (or, as he usually expressed it in the vulgar Marxism current at the time, the "workers"), it is surprising how little sustained attention Maritain gave to the most significant new
discipline of postmedieval times, political economy, with the
accent on *economy.* Maritain came to the problems of politics
and society rather late in his reflections and then, having achieved
much, never took up a study of the great economic classics,

especially those of the Austrian and Anglo-American worlds, not even of such French writers as Bastiat. Further, much as he admired the United States—a civilization, he felt, full of reverberations of the realities to which he was trying to point in *Integral Humanism*[1] — Maritain never really grappled with such classics of American political economy as *The Federalist, Democracy in America* (by his fellow Frenchman Alexis de Tocqueville), and the works of Abraham Lincoln. He did suggest that treasures of the human spirit lay buried there, but we never received the benefit of his sustained reflection on them.

On the whole, Maritain wrote a beautiful prose, a prose that reaches the heart and the imagination more than that of most philosophers, while manifesting as well a Thomist love of exquisite clarity, particularly in the making of distinctions (often made more precise by other distinctions). To read him is to be forced to look, through such distinctions, from many angles of vision at once. And all for the sake of unity: "To distinguish in order to unite" was a most suitable motto for his life's work. He had a passion for clear and precise ideas, distinguished sharply from their nearest neighbors, as well as for the relations that tie each idea to every other. Sometimes, indeed, he tried to capture too much in one sentence, piling up distinctions within distinctions or introducing an aside about some analogous matter, while trying to capture a whole *gestalt*. Many of his sentences must be reread. The effort is almost always worth it, for his true conversational partners were less his contemporary critics than the classics, whose precise treasures he did not wish to muffle, to encrust, or to belittle by oversimplification.

The Intuition of Being

In the autumn of 1960, in one of my very first conversations with a full professor in Harvard's philosophy department, a teacher of metaphysics and ethics who confessed cheerily that he deeply admired Hume's happy atheism, mentioned to me, nonetheless, how deeply impressed he had been with Jacques Maritain during the latter's presence on campus. "He was perhaps the most saintly philosopher I have ever known," he said to me, "gentle, kind, honest, almost childlike. Of course, I didn't agree with a single position he took. But I did come to admire him a great deal." This was meant to be a warning to me, of course; I should not expect an easy time at Harvard. Yet it was also meant as a token of esteem for a significant tradition and a remarkable thinker: no small tribute in those days.

Professor Williams' tribute to Maritain's saintliness, his gentleness, his childlike manner has remained with me, especially the unusual word (for Harvard) *childlike*. This is, I think, the key to Maritain's intuition of being, in which so many other philosophers simply could not follow him. Maritain approached each day with a certain wonder — at the color of the sky, the scent of the grass, the feel of the breeze. He marveled that such a world could have come to be. There was no necessity in its coming to be. It had happened. Here it was. He could sense it, his every sensible organ alive to its active solicitations of color, sound, scent, taste, and feel. More than that, his intellect would wonder at it, knowing that it did not have to be as it was on that particular day, or on any other day. And it could also cease to be.

Well before the cloudburst of the first atomic bomb, long before a perceived "ecological crisis", Maritain perceived the fragility of earth — not only in his personal mortality (born on November 18, 1882, Maritain had lived long before he visited Harvard; he was to die in 1973); not only, either, in the fragility of planet earth. Rather, Maritain sensed, in the obscure way of the human intellect at its most childlike and most profound, that all changeable created things — all things short of an existent necessarily and fully existing in itself — are fragile and dependent. My professors at Harvard found this intuition difficult to grasp or, rather, even on its brink profoundly resisted it. I remember one seminar on the existence of God, taught by

Professor Rogers Albritton, a student of Wittgenstein's who imported many of Wittgenstein's legendary mannerisms into our classroom, when Professor Albritton was diagramming on the blackboard Aquinas' way to the existence of God from contingency and necessity. The good professor, an honest man so far as he could go, kept pointing to the major and minor premises, one after the other, and then confessed that he could find no notion of "necessity" that made the argument flow into Aquinas' conclusion. He then tried to supply all the definitions of "necessity" known to him. None would work. I remember quite clearly summoning up my courage and raising my hand. It was about twenty minutes before class was to adjourn. Nervously, I reminded him (Professor Albritton also taught Aristotle) that, based upon a rudimentary (and now recognized to be false) empirical observation, Aristotle and Aquinas thought that the stars in the firmament were unchangeable, permanent, and thus, in a special sense, "necessary beings", different from all other changeable substances they had observed. Suppose, I hesitantly said, this gave them a warrant for speaking empirically of "necessary beings". And suppose, further, that they postulated still other necessary beings, in a different class, not composed of material properties at all, yet nonetheless not contingent, not changeable, but beings-in-themselves, which, once existing, never ceased to exist. Suppose, further, that such necessary beings could cause the coming into existence of the contingent beings of whose existence we had no doubt. All these suppositions might be false, I remember saying. Still, if Aristotle and Aquinas held them (and clearly the texts make plain that they did), then, looking again at the premises on the board, doesn't the conclusion suddenly flow? Professor Albritton rubbed his chin Wittgenstein-style and looked again at the board. "Hmmm", he said. "Good point." He looked at his watch. "Well, let's think about that until next time." The class adjourned early. We never went back to the argument from contingency. Perhaps Professor Albritton wished to be merciful.

Young as I was, I had no illusions that suddenly Harvard

would reach the conclusion that, indeed, mysterious and terri-
fying as it may be, there is (or even could be) a necessary existent
that explains how this fragile world of change and contingency
could come to be and, perhaps, to perish. No one had any problem contemplating some Big Bang or "happening to come to
be"; nor, at least in later years, does anyone have severe doubts
that, whether with Bang or Whimper, this fragile world of ours
could cease to be. The *hard* thing to accept, it seems, is that
there is an existent not doomed to our changeability, on whom
our existence depends. (Why should that be so hard, I won-
dered, since so many billions of human beings have always believed it? Life for Harvard philosophers, however, is more
difficult than for others, and nobody ever said it was not.)

   A childlike grown-up, however, aware of no special need
to see the world as a Harvard philosopher does, could not help
being struck by the marvel that no one denies: that things mar-
velously *are* and then *are not.* The fragility of all beings that we
encounter is all too well known to the sensitive intellect. This
sharp taste of fragile existence, to begin with, is "the intuition
of being" — or, to be more precise, since the one word *being* is
sometimes used of more than one aspect of reality, "the intuition of existing". Allow me to dwell for a moment on the difference between the essential characteristics and the existing of
things. The air outside as I write is a cool, fresh October air,
blown in from Canada, whereas yesterday's air, blown in from
the Caribbean, was muggy and moist. It is not their *coolness*
and their *mugginess* that so much attract my attention, at moments, as the fact that one is and the other was but is not and
the sure knowledge that the one that today is will also pass
away. So it is also with the pen so comfortable now in my
fingers, and with this narrow-lined paper on which I write and
soon (once the typescript is prepared) to be thrown away, and
with my very fingers themselves. All will return to dust. Yet
today they gloriously *are,* and the taste of that existing is so
keen that it sometimes makes one wish to exult and to break
into glories: "It is such a glorious day!"

I do not wish to confuse this insight into existing with the further inference (although it seems to me almost instantaneous) that I should thank someone, something, some glory, for the lucky break of existing. These are two separate movements of the soul. Yet the most salient one, surely, if only because for us it is the first, is the intuition of the sheer existing of fragile, unnecessary things. (Had I died on the numerous occasions when I am aware of almost having done so, the particular existents mentioned above would never have been; had my parents never given me birth, or their parents them . . . so easily would the world never have missed these fragile existents.)

Nonetheless, I am emboldened by the recent testimony of my second favorite atheist humanist, Sidney Hook—Albert Camus still being my first—who just before his death confided to the American Jewish Committee Archives that there were many times in his life, at the height of his powers, that he often felt well up within him the desire to say thanks that things, which might have gone badly, worked out in existence as they had.[2] This barely conscious, intuitive inference seems to me wholly natural. It seems to me also a bit of data about the human intellect that ought never to be lost to the attention of philosophers. Sidney Hook was a supremely honest man, willing to put on the record evidence that went against his own philosophy. True, he not only never interpreted that bit of data as Maritain did but also, given many opportunities to confront interpretations of human life such as Maritain's, never accepted them. That bit of data about the movement of human intellect to utter thanks, nonetheless, remains to be explained.

On Social and Political Reconstruction

It is not my intention, however, to spell out the implications that Maritain derived from his intuition of the existent, not at least in the direction of metaphysics, the philosophy of God, or even Jewish and Christian faith. (Maritain was deeply involved, through his marriage with Raïssa, in questions of Jewish as well as Christian faith; in fact, he may have done as much as any Christian in our time to lay the intellectual groundwork for a special instinct of fraternity among Christians and Jews.) I would prefer for today to carry the intuition of the existent into Maritain's further reflections on politics and society.

For if all of human existence is fragile, even more fragile is human action, above all in the political sphere. Maritain writes in *Existence and the Existent* that the end of practical wisdom is "not to know that which exists but to cause to exist what is not yet".[3] Between the cup and the lip, many a slip. It is easier to intend results in ethical or in political action than to achieve those results. Politics, in a language more favored by Reinhold Niebuhr than by Maritain but by no means in conflict with the latter's, is the realm of the contingent, the ironic, and the tragic.

Allow me to pause for a moment to observe the sharp difference between a Thomist view of politics, such as that of Maritain, and that, say, of classical conservatives such as Russell Kirk. Struck by the contingency and organic relatedness of social institutions, practices, and actions, and dismayed by the utopian ideologies to which so many modern minds are prone, paleoconservatives (so they now style themselves) such as Kirk are opposed to "ideological infatuation" or even to imagining social projects for the future at all.[4] Considering the projection of social notions into the future to be signs of the disease of "ideology", such conservatives prefer to let things continue, to move along "organically", to be. They resist "thinking for the future", for fear of contamination by ideology.

Maritain had a significantly different view. By its very nature, for him (as for Thomas Aquinas, "the first Whig"),[5] practical intellect is aimed not at knowing that which already exists but at causing to exist what is not yet. Practical intellect is by its very nature oriented toward the future and, precisely, to changing the future, to making the future different, "to cause to exist what does not yet exist". For this reason, Maritain did not hesitate in *Integral Humanism* (1936) to imagine proximate probable futures or to suggest new courses of action that would alter the awful European present of the World War II era in the light of a better—and more humane, more Christian— proximate future.

Maritain took considerable care not to think in a merely utopian fashion. But he did not hesitate to try to imagine proximate, achievable next steps, which might in turn lead to yet further achievable steps, toward building up a more humane and more Christian civilization than the world had yet known. In brief, Maritain shared with those Whigs who are currently known as "neoconservatives" a willingness to project a future more attractive than socialists or others were imagining, and yet a future thoroughly realizable within the bounds of proximate probable judgments. Unlike Kirk, Maritain was not willing to embrace mere social laissez-faire in the political realm, and he was resolutely opposed to mere nostalgia about some supposedly more humane premodern era. Maritain claimed the future. Indeed, insofar as the Christian Democratic parties of Sturzo, de Gasperi, Schuman, and Adenauer draw crucial inspiration from his work, Maritain may be said, in fact, to have caused to exist much that had not existed before him.

In this sense, Aquinas is properly called the "first Whig" because his ethic and his politics did lay claims upon the future; did inspire, down the ages, a search for political institutions worthy of the rational, consensual dignity of humans. This is the sense in which Maritain was able in *Christianity and Democracy, Man and the State,* and other works to claim for a specific idea of democracy the support of the main spine of the Christian intellectual tradition. For this tradition nourished over the centuries the slow emergence of the ideal of a civilized politics, a politics of civil conversation, of noncoercion, of the consent of the governed, of pluralism, of religious liberty, of respect for the inalienable dignity of every human person, of voluntary cooperation in pursuit of the common good, and of checks and balances against the wayward tendencies of sinful men and women. Here, as will become clear in a moment, Maritain did not claim too much for the historical efficacy of the Christian intellectual tradition; he chastised its failures severely and gave credit to nonbelievers for crucial advances. But neither did he wish to claim too little.

Here, too, it is necessary to see how profound was Maritain's grasp of the hold that the ideal of *caritas* had upon the political thinking of Thomas Aquinas. Maritain held that action in the world—whether ethical action among individuals or political action among systems, institutions, and groups— is always action among *existents,* among real sinners and saints and all those in between, not among purely "rational agents". For him, realistic thinking about ethics and politics could not be conducted wholly within the boundaries of philosophy; theology was necessarily required. Why is this so? It is so because ethics and politics are about the real, existing world, and in this existing world humans are not purely rational agents but, rather, fallen creatures who are potentially redeemed by grace, on the condition that they are willing to accept God's action within them. To proceed in merely philosophical categories about ethics and politics would be merely utopian; one must deal with real, existing creatures locked in the actual historical drama of sin and grace.[6]

That is why, in explicating "the fundamentally existential character of Thomist ethics", Maritain stresses two points, one regarding charity, the other regarding practical wisdom or prudence. Concerning the first, he writes:

> St. Thomas teaches that perfection consists in charity, and that each of us is bound to tend toward the perfection of love according to his condition and in so far as it is in his power. All morality thus hangs upon that which is most existential in the world. For love (this is another Thomist theme) does not deal with possibles or pure essences, it deals with existents. We do not love possibles, we love that which exists or is destined to exist.[7]

Regarding practical wisdom, Maritain makes two extremely subtle points, whose fullness I will not be able to reproduce. The first is that, at the heart of concrete existence, when a real, concrete person is confronted with a set of particulars amid which to decide to act, that person's appetite—that person's will or secret and deepest loves—enters into the quality of her or his perception of alternatives. More than that, for Aquinas, the rectitude of an existing person's intellect depends upon the rectitude of his existing loves. This is a powerfully realistic doctrine. Intellect follows love, and if the love is errant, so also will be the judgment of practical intellect or "conscience". Although, for Maritain as for Aquinas, practical intellect still exerts a major discipline over the soul (over its loves, for example), nonetheless, *here and now,* under the immediate pressures of choice, the predispositions of one's loves are highly likely to bend the intellect to their purposes. (Were not David Hume and Adam Smith, under different background assumptions but with the same Augustinian sense for real experience, to make an analogous point?)

Hence, for Aquinas, there is necessary in one's ethical formation in advance of such choices a deep and profound habit of disciplining and directing one's loves, seducing them, so to speak, so that in every case love will be of the good, the true, and the just, and be habituated to being restless with anything less. Absent a right will, a right practical intelligence will also be absent. In doing what they think is best, those whose loves are disordered will distort even their own intellects. As they love, so will they perceive. "Love is blind", we say, meaning that, disordered, it is more powerful than light, obscures the light, and darkens the eye of intelligence itself.

The second subtle point that Maritain makes about practical intellect begins again with the fact that ethical and political action is always about existents. This time he points out that such action always faces two wholly singular, irrepeatable realities: first, the singular character, here and now, of this particular

agent; and, second, the singular, never-to-be-repeated circumstances of the here and now. For these two reasons, practical
wisdom is utterly different from science. Whereas scientific
judgment depends upon regularities, moral judgment must cope
with singulars. "The same moral case never appears twice in
the world. To speak absolutely strictly, precedent does not exist."[8] Practical wisdom concerns unprecedented singulars ("Useless to thumb through the dictionary of cases of conscience!"),
on the one hand. On the other hand, its point is "not to know
that which exists, but to cause that to exist which is not yet",
and so it is moved by the appetite of will or love, which thrusts
us toward creating something new, either of evil or of good.

On a Specific Idea of Democracy

From this discussion of the sheer existing of ethical and political action — *here and now,* singular, unprecedented, irrepeatable —
it follows, *in nuce,* that building a humane, Christian society
is an iffy business. It cannot be built upon any institutional
framework at all; it has preconditions; many things can go
wrong. Thus, to be faithful to the full measure of Christian
intellectual conviction about the dignity (and fallibility) of the
human person, about civilization as a state of society characterized by uncoerced decisions arrived at through civil discourse, and about the pull upon human love of God's own
command of love, new forms of social institutions will have
to be labored toward in history, and not without setbacks. For
reasons Maritain articulates at some length, a certain kind of
democracy, guarded against the diseases to which "pure" democracies are prey, best represents the full flowering of human practical wisdom about the sorts of institutions worthy
of Jewish and Christian thought. This particular kind of democratic reality gives the broken world of the Second World War
some hope for a better future.

Maritain is not unsophisticated about democracy. He knows,

writing in 1944 in the depths of destruction, that "the very name democracy has a different ring in America and in Europe".[9] And, before proceeding very far on this subject, in *Christianity and Democracy*, Maritain makes three important distinctions, each of which he discusses at more length than we can here duplicate: "First, the word democracy, as used by modern peoples, has a wider meaning than in the classical treatises on the science of government. It designates first and foremost a general philosophy of human and political life."[10] Its inner dynamism, although consistent with a monarchic regime and even other classic "regimes" or "forms of government", leads, "in the words of Abraham Lincoln", to "government of the people, by the people, for the people". Democratic regimes are not the only good regimes, but all good regimes will have to embody the dynamism of respect for free persons and their consent.

Second, democracy after the war will certainly have to be constitutional democracy, based on constitutions that have at least three characteristics: formation through the consent of the governed; protection of "the essential bases of common life, respect for human dignity and the rights of the person"; and grounding in a "long process of education". This long process of education will be necessary to lead peoples away from habits of dictatorship, nationalistic impulses, and the mental habits of unfree and coercively minded peoples. It will have to lead them toward the "slow and difficult construction" of new habits in the temporal life of nations, supportive of "the soul of democracy" — that is, "the law of brotherly love and the spiritual dignity of the person".

By these first two distinctions, Maritain shows that he means what in the United States we mean by a democratic republic, protective of the rights of the person. He means no totalitarian or merely majoritarian democracy, but limited government, grounded in a tradition of sound habits, associations, and institutions. Moreover, he means a set of principles not exhausted by any one form of regime, and yet capable of distinguishing false from true ideas of democracy. Then, by his third distinction, Maritain makes clear both that Christian faith cannot be made subservient to democracy as a philosophy of life and that democracy cannot claim to be the only form of regime demanded by Christian belief. He means "by no means to pretend that Christianity is linked to democracy and that Christian faith compels every Christian to be a democrat".[11] To do so would be to mix the things of Caesar and the things of God. Nonetheless, Maritain does affirm "that democracy is linked to Christianity and that the democratic impulse has arisen in human history as a temporal manifestation of the inspiration of the Gospel".

Yet Maritain does not say that Christianity exists in the world solely as the Church or the body of believers. Rather, he sees "Christianity as historical energy at work in the world. It is not in the heights of theology, it is in the depths of the secular conscience and secular existence that Christianity works in this fashion." He is equally far from asserting that Christians brought modern democratic institutions into existence: "It was not given to believers in Catholic dogma but to rationalists to proclaim in France the rights of man and of the citizen, to Puritans to strike the last blow at slavery in America."[12] He gives credit — by schematic suggestion, not comprehensive detail — where credit is due: "Neither Locke nor Jean-Jacques Rousseau nor the Encyclopedists can pass as thinkers faithful to the integrity of the Christian trust."[13]

Thus, here again, Maritain is interested in existents, not essences. In the existing world of 1944, "The chances of religion, conscience and civilization coincide with those of freedom; freedom's chances coincide with those of the evangelical message."[14] The terrors of war have obliged the democracies to rethink their spiritual foundations, so as to recover their spiritual energies and humanizing mission. They dare not go back to what they were before. The demands of the human spirit in our time include authentic demands, many of them rooted in the Gospels and in the deepest Christian intellectual traditions about the nature of human existents. These have not always been expressed best, or developed in practical life, by believers. It is clear that Maritain considers the Christian message about the cry of the poor for justice to be a motor of human temporal life. He holds simultaneously that existing democratic ideas, traditions, and institutions were often championed in actual history by those who were non-Christians or even anti-Christian; and yet that, in building better than they knew, such persons were often generating in human temporal life important constructs whose foundations were not only consistent with Jewish and Christian convictions about the realities of ethical and political life but, in a sense, dependent on them. Pull out from under genuine democratic principles the beliefs of Judaism and Christianity about the transcendent dignity of the person and the human propensity to sin, and the existing edifice of democratic thought is exposed to radical doubt.

Thus, Maritain argued further that existing democratic institutions need to be grounded on a deeper, sounder foundation of intellectual conviction and moral habits than had so far been wrought in actual history. He urged Christians to take up this work, both in intellect and in active practice. He saw a great deal to be done in the "slow and difficult construction" of a more humane world, whether considered from a Christian or a humanistic viewpoint. He saw this task as both intellectual and moral.

A Salute

Perhaps I have said enough to show why so many of us feel immensely indebted to this layman, perhaps the greatest exemplar of the Catholic laity in the last two centuries: this master of many wisdoms, this metaphysician, this philosopher at once humane and Christian (and able to speak in either of those languages), this ethicist and philosopher of history, this political philosopher, this saintly and childlike man.

Jacques Maritain, approaching the 107th anniversary of your

birth, we salute you. And with the thanks that Sidney Hook often felt the impulse to utter, we thank the Creator of all existents for your brief presence among us. May you and Sidney, and all the just and righteous philosophers, enjoy that endless pursuit of Truth, face to face, which you conducted so lovingly on this fragile earth.

NOTES

[1] "I hope you will pardon me if I now seem to give a more personal turn to my reflections. The fact is that I would like to refer to one of my books, *Humanisme intégral,* which was published twenty years ago. When I wrote this book, trying to outline a concrete historical ideal suitable to a new Christian civilization, my perspective was definitely European. I was in no way thinking in American terms, I was thinking especially of France, and of Europe, and of their historical problems, and of the kind of concrete prospective image that might inspire the activity, in the temporal field, of the Catholic youth of my country.

"The curious thing in this connection is that, fond as I may have been of America as soon as I saw her, and probably because of the particular perspective in which *Humanisme intégral* was written, it took a rather long time for me to become aware of the kind of congeniality which existed between what is going on in this country and a number of views I had expressed in my book.

"Of course the book is concerned with a concrete historical ideal which is far distant from any present reality. Yet what matters to me is the direction of certain essential trends characteristic of American civilization. And from this point of view I may say that *Humanisme intégral* appears to me now as a book which had, so to speak, an affinity with the American climate by anticipation" (Jacques Maritain, *Reflections on America* [New York: Scribner's, 1958], pp. 174–75).

[2] See "On Being a Jew", an interview with Norman Podhoretz, *Commentary,* Oct. 1989, p. 30.

[3] Jacques Maritain, *Existence and the Existent,* trans. Lewis Galantière and Gerald B. Phelan (Garden City, N.Y.: Doubleday, Image Books, 1956), p. 59.

[4] See Russell Kirk's lecture "The Neoconservatives: An Endangered Species", delivered at the Heritage Foundation, Washington, D.C., on Oct. 6, 1988, pp. 5–7. It has been distributed as *Heritage Lecture* No. 178.

[5] Commenting on an early medieval text, Lord Acton remarked: "This language, which contains the earliest exposition of the Whig theory of revolution, is taken from the works of St. Thomas Aquinas" (Lord Acton, "The History of Freedom in Antiquity", in *Essays on Freedom and Power,* ed. Gertrude Himmelfarb [Cleveland and New York: World Publishing Co., 1955], p. 88). Embracing for himself the term *Whig,* Friedrich A. Hayek remarks that "in some respects Lord Acton was not being altogether paradoxical when he described Thomas Aquinas as the First Whig" (*The Constitution of Liberty* [Chicago: University of Chicago Press, 1960], p. 457, n. 4; see also the discussion of the Whigs in the Postscript, "Why I Am Not a Conservative", pp. 397–414).

⁶ Maritain elaborates thus: "Because of the fundamentally existential character of Thomist moral philosophy — however vast, necessary, and fundamental be the part that natural ethics plays in it — a moral philosophy adequately taken, that is, a moral philosophy really apt to guide action, is conceivable in such a philosophy only if it takes into account the existential state of humanity, with all the wounds or weaknesses and all the resources that it comprises in fact; and if, therefore, it takes into account the higher data of theology (as well as the data of ethnology and sociology)." Cf. J. Maritain, *Science et Sagesse,* pp. 228–362, Eng. trans., pp. 138–220 (Maritain, *Existence and the Existent,* p. 58, n. 2).

⁷ Ibid., p. 58.

⁸ Ibid., p. 60.

⁹ "In America, where, despite the influence wielded by the great economic interests, democracy has penetrated more profoundly into existence, and where it has never lost sight of its Christian origin, this name conjures up a living instinct stronger than the errors of the spirit which prey upon it. In Europe it conjures up an ideal scoffed at by reality, and whose soul has been half devoured by these same errors" (Jacques Maritain, *Christianity and Democracy* [San Francisco: Ignatius Press, 1986], p. 23).

¹⁰ Ibid., p. 33.

¹¹ Ibid., p. 37.

¹² Ibid., p. 38.

¹³ Ibid., p. 40.

¹⁴ Ibid., p. 41.

FREDERICK D. WILHELMSEN

HILAIRE BELLOC:
DEFENDER OF THE FAITH

Had we had ten Hilaire Bellocs in the English-speaking Catholic world in the past fifty years, we might have converted the whole kit-and-caboodle and avoided the mess we find ourselves in today. With that impossible declaration behind me, I might better begin with a story told about him—he was a man who collected myths about his person, and I cannot verify the truth of this. Upon being honored with a papal decoration well into his old age, Belloc refused to put out the money needed to buy the medal and grumbled: "What would they say if I changed my mind?"

Hilaire Belloc was not built to fit any cloth fashioned by mortal man. Although he often groused about his own age (I do not mean his chronological age—he always complained about that!—but his moment in time), Belloc would have been impossible in any other age. Growing up as he did, in the twilight of the reign of Queen Victoria, blinking brilliantly in nonsense verse and radical politics in the time of King Edward VII, a child prodigy called by his aunt "Old Thunder", Hilaire Belloc reposed upon a broad upper-middle-class English society that read him, first adored him, then good-naturedly put up with him, and finally isolated him. "I was once welcome in that house", he commented wistfully when the automobile in which he was driving passed the home of an exceedingly rich man. His intransigent defense of all things Catholic first amused a literate and basically skeptical gentry looking for novelty; then offended; finally, it was considered intolerable.

A. N. Wilson in his biography of Belloc wrote: "If I created a character in a novel as Hilaire Belloc, people would not believe it." Belloc was a paradox: a lyrical poet who never read any contemporary poetry; a rhymester whose high jinks still charm children; an artilleryman on bivouac at Toul who smelled the Revolution as "France went by"; an aging monarchist who savored the last charge of Charles I at Naseby; the most versatile and certainly the finest English prose stylist in this and possibly any century, who grumbled from the liberty of his battered old boat, the Nona, "dear reader, read less and sail more" even as he lusted for bigger and better-paying audiences; the perpetual wanderer tramping Europe, burning for adventures even as he sang the praises of a rooted peasantry and a hearth steeped in seasonable traditions that "halted the cruelty of time"; the enemy of the rich and of capitalist greed, who once asked for a bucket of money as a birthday gift; the passionate advocate of Truth, who once groused, however, "that the truth always limps"; the drummer boy of an English-speaking Catholicism he helped make proud of itself.

At my last count, Hilaire Belloc wrote 153 books. The business has to do with vigor, an enormous lust for life, and a willingness to make mistakes. Belloc did not give a damn for what anybody thought of him. He wrote his life of King James II in a hotel on the edge of the Sahara in ten days: "It is full of howlers and is the fruit of liberty." He walked to Rome as a young man, coming in upon the Appian Way on a mule-drawn cart—but with his feet dragging on the road so his vow would not be broken.

His vigor was legendary, and I have mentioned as well his lust for life. Belloc—and this is a key to understanding his role as a Catholic apologist—was a man totally at home in this world, but one who knew it was an illusion to be so at home. There was not a trace of Manicheanism in him, and he called puritanism, in his biography of Louis XIV, an "evil out of the pit", meaning the pit of hell. A mountain climber, he was even more a sailor. His *Hills and the Sea* and *The Cruise of the Nona* are classics. If *The Path to Rome* is the work of a young genius, rollicking and rolling his way over mountain and valley toward the Eternal City, *The Four Men,* on the contrary, called by its author "A Farrago", was penned in solitude mixed with melancholy. Grizzlebeard, the Poet, and the Sailor are all extensions of Myself, and Myself is Belloc. Only when life is lived close to the senses, when the intelligence is engaged immediately on what is yielded to man through the body, is the paradox of sadness in created beauty brought home in all its delicacy and inexorableness. Page after page of Belloc's writing is troubled by a deep and troubled gravity, heightened by his profound communion with the things of his world: English inns; old oak—burnished and sturdy; rich Burgundy and other wines— "that port of theirs" at the "George" drunk by the fire with which he began this book; the sea and ships that sail—but, please, "no abomination of an engine"; the smell of the tides. These loves run through Belloc's essays, recurring themes testifying to a vision movingly poetic in its classic simplicity. His eyes are fixed on the primal things that always nourished the human spirit, on the things at hand. He wrote:

> Every pleasure I know comes from an intimate union between my body and my very human mind, which last receives, confirms, revives, and can summon up again what my body has experienced. Of pleasures, however, in which my senses have no part, I know nothing.

It was this very man, rooted in this world and not in the next, who was to become the first defender of the Catholic Church in England during his lifetime. A key to his understanding of things spiritual was his vivid awareness that all things good pass, that life is filled with what Allan Tate called "rumors of mortality". In an essay named "Harbour in the North", Belloc brings his little cutter under a long seawall, and there meets another small vessel. The pilot declares that he is off to find a permanent refuge to the north in a harbor of whose fame he has heard. "In that place I shall discover again such full moments of content as I have known, and I shall preserve them without failing." The stranger, of course, is Belloc's Sailor; and Myself, Belloc himself, answers from his own boat—the Ship of Mortality—"You cannot make the harbour . . . . It is not of this world."

An almost savage realism mixed with Belloc's sensibility, and his meditations on death are the most moving in all English letters. Read of the execution of Danton, written in the fires of early youth; of the murder of King Charles I; of the death-bed conversion of King Charles II; and, finally, in his *Elizabethan Commentary,* one of his last books, Belloc reveals himself: "She felt that she was ceasing to be herself and that is what probably most of us will feel when the moment comes to reply to the summons of Azrael." Belloc's emotional skepticism is at its purest in an essay called "Cornetto of the Tarquins" in his *Towns of Destiny.* Speaking of those tombs which are of the origins of us all, he tells us of "the subterranean vision of death, the dusk of religion, which they imposed on Rome and from which we all inherit—then as I thought to myself, as I looked westward from the wall, how man might say of the life of all our race as of the life of one, that we know not whence it came, nor whither it goes". Confessing himself to be of a skeptical mind, in a famous letter to Chesterton on the occasion of Chesterton's conversion, Belloc's skepticism was conquered by his faith, but the temptation to despair remained with him all his life. To me, this has always seemed strange because Heideggerian angst and dread before the specter of the Nothing seem the peculiar and often awful temptations of those with a metaphysical bent of mind—and Belloc had none at all. In *The Cruise of the Nona,* he wrote "of the metaphysic . . . who can see it and who can bite into it? It is of no use whatsoever." Altogether without philosophical preoccupations, he was nonetheless haunted by the temptation that at bottom there is no answer to the riddle of human existence. His conquest of that aberration made his faith something hard, crystal clear, without compromise. Of religions other than the Catholic he had an Olympian contempt and an impatience only barely disguised and then imperfectly. He would not have fared well in these days of ecumenical tea parties, and the so-called New Church would have bewildered him. Belloc frequently took pains to point out that tolerance is always of a lesser evil that cannot be vanquished at the moment, but vanquished it ought to be.

From whence, then, came his lyrical Catholicism, for which he was to sacrifice fame, all possibility of wealth—Belloc died a poor man—and every avenue—there were many of them—for a public career in politics? Born and baptized in the Church, a Catholic from childhood, his love and appreciation of the Faith came to him when young, but it came somewhat slowly. Of his inner life he tells us very little. French on his father's side, Belloc—it must be remembered—did his military service in the French artillery, thus delaying his entrance into Oxford when he finally made up his mind to remain an Englishman. His spoken French remained that of a rough cannoneer. Latin European culture was the air he breathed in his youth and to which he returned whenever he could, even sailing across the channel to replenish his reserves of wine.

Were I to seek one scriptural passage which sums up Belloc's vision of the Faith, it would be: "By their fruits ye shall know them" (Mt 6:30). Aided here by a powerful visual imagination which was brought to bear in his many military histories, Belloc could see the Church at work down the ages—and he adored what he saw. The Church made Europe and in so doing quickened the old Roman Order, in disrepair but by no means destroyed by the Germanic tribes from the north. All our typical Western institutions were either created by Catholic men from out of nothing or were inherited from our pagan forefathers and then quickened from within by the yeast of Christianity. Although the terms *incarnational* and *eschatological* were not current in Belloc's lifetime, he is a prime instance of a man with an incarnational understanding of religious truth. Belloc looked for blessings everywhere, and the whole of Christendom was for him an immense network of actual graces.

Making his own the Thomistic insistence that grace perfects nature, the inheritance of classical antiquity, he maintained, was preserved and transfigured in the fires of Faith. In our world — at least as Belloc knew it in what might have been its twilight: the subject is foreign to my paper today — men achieved a free peasantry that marked the whole of Europe for centuries. In that *ordo orbis,* justice flourished and free men discovering thus their liberty exercised it through two millennia in the creation of a culture that Belloc once called "the standing grace of this world". There we all experienced not only a free citizenry but the sacredness of marriage, the dignity of men, chivalry, the steady rejection of Manichean irresponsibility and of every pantheist negation, the sacramental universe. These are to be found in Catholic Europe and wherever else she has stamped her genius, and are to be found as corporate doctrines tending to actuality nowhere else on this earth.

Belloc understood a rooted life, close to nature, as being humanly superior to the massification produced by modern civilization. Give a man a farm, a small business, an artisan's anvil, a boat to sail, wine to drink — suffuse all this with the love of Christ; center man's life around liturgical rhythms; and that man — at least Man writ in the large and taken by the handful — is happier than his industrial counterpart. A Catholic culture tends — and *tends* is the operative word — toward this kind of life. Tempering greed and avarice, man is then more than himself. As A. N. Wilson notes, in his introduction to a new edition of *The Four Men,* Belloc knew that his ideal was doomed, and his only consolation was an unholy glee in letting everybody else know that the world was going to hell: "I told you so."

Hilaire Belloc, spreading his many talents and his incredible energy through the essay, a respectable body of very good verse, military history, nonsense novels, biography and books of travel, studies on the road, political polemics, economic theory, concentrated it all into a center, into a synthesized focus: the apostolate of history. *Credo in unam, sanctam, apostolicam eccelesiam,* we all recite — but Belloc took the note of apostolicity seriously. I do not mean this in the sense that Belloc showed a lively interest in controversy concerning the apostolic succession. He took that as a settled issue: *Roma locuta est, causa finita.* I mean it rather in the sense that he understood himself to be a man called to be an apostle. Ronald Knox, in his panegyric at Belloc's grave site, called him more a prophet than an apostle. Possibly both Knox and I are right because Hilaire Belloc was a missionary in Protestant England, and his principal weapon was history. I doubt that this was a conscious decision, a free act exercised at one crucial moment in his life. By temperament and talent, Belloc was an historian. He soon concluded, shortly after his disillusion with parliamentary politics (he served two terms, one as a Liberal and one as an Independent), that the English-speaking world had been lied to about its past and about its present, that this lie was bound up with the Protestant establishment, which officially dates from 1689 but which in fact reached far deeper into the English past.

Agreeing with Cobbett (whom, however, he rarely cited and who apparently had little direct influence on him: the two men converged in their historical judgment) that the Protestant Reformation "was the rising of the rich against the poor", Belloc unpacked layer after layer of "official history" and turned over its foundation, a Great Lie. The religious zealotry of a handful of heretics was used by the mercantile and landed classes of England, aided by the lust of Henry VIII, to abolish the old Catholic Order. If Belloc had any real enemy, it was the Whigs. Of the Earl of Shaftsbury, he wrote: "He is probably in hell." William of Orange he called that "little pervert" — and, of course, the man was just that! Although Belloc never quoted Samuel Johnson's famous "The Devil was the first Whig", the whole weight of Belloc's historical writing yields the same conclusion. But although Belloc loathed the Whigs, he had little in common with the Tories. A populist Catholic radical, a burned-out republican by middle age, a man chastened into royalism, he would have been out with Bonnie Prince Charlie in the '45.

Time prohibits my detailing Belloc's revolution in English historical writing. Suffice it to say — and this is said formally and altogether without rhetorical emphasis — that one man, Hilaire Belloc, turned the whole writing of British history around. Since Belloc, nobody can get away with understanding the Reformation as the work of high-minded souls bent on liberty and democracy, noble souls who brought England out of the darkness of Catholic superstition and medieval obscurantism. Others footnoted Belloc and traded on his vision. They did well in doing so, but the vision was his — as was the persecution of silence that followed on his work.

If by their fruits ye shall know them, then the fruits of the Revolt against Rome have been sufficiently documented; more important, they have so pained the bones of all of us that to know them well is to revolt against the Revolt. Men were cheapened in their dignity. They cringed Calvinistically under a cruel and implacable God who damned most of them from all eternity to hell, and who filled the barns of the saved. The beauty and grandeur, even languor, of an old order of things gave way to a severity and grimness of style and manner that choked off man's natural response to the beauty of the world God had created. Belloc would have none of it, and he exposed the fraud. Behind the psalm-singing fanatics, there reposes the weight of what he called The Money Power, the new Capitalism and Banking System, that enslaved Europe to its greed. Belloc detailed it all in lavish description in book after book — toward the end, he was repeating himself. If his prose never bored, his arguments often did. The modern world, built on money and heresy, has had and has as its enemy the Catholic Church and the Order she has created. Quite clearly, Mr. Belloc, as he was called in his old age, did not like the modern world — gray, anonymous, bereft of beauty, craftmanship ignorant of nobility, shorn of dignity. Yet, as already noted, the England of his own time was probably the only place he could have flourished as he did. Winston Churchill offered him a high honor, in the name of the king, in the twilight of Belloc's life, when the bombs were bursting over Britain. Belloc turned him down courteously.

Cardinal Ratzinger wrote, in a piece about liturgy a short time ago, that the only apologetic the Church has for her truth are her saints and her art. Neither are to be found anywhere else within the broad sweep of man's adventure through time as they are in the Church. Belloc, I think, would have agreed in part with the cardinal. How often did our author pause before tower and church, the easy grace of French and English villages unspoiled by industrialism, as they broke upon vision at dawn and then heightened and blessed the woods and hills surrounding them? How often did he not speak of the Cathedral of Seville as the first marvel of Western art—and this from a man French and not Spanish in temperament? And did he not write the finest panegyric to Saint Joan of Arc—none is better— and do it in an English that matched the French of her own time? No: if the Faith be not the answer to the human heart, then there is none. But Belloc would probably have added to Ratzinger's saints and art the entire social order brought into being by men who sensed, often obscurely, that if Christ were not in the marketplace, he was nowhere. And this, I hasten to add, from a man who held that the center of existence was the tabernacle of the altar. Those close to him have witnessed to his deepening devotion to the Eucharist as the years bent him down. Indeed, Belloc insisted, it was the hatred for and attack on transubstantiation that formed the center of the bitterness moving the English reformers in the sixteenth century. Read Belloc on Cranmer. They turned all the altars around and made of them tables and thus first obscured and finally denied what it is that gave life to Catholic churches and left all others temples reminiscent of tombs.

Faith is to be fought for and, once won—if won only precariously—cherished and watered, but not watered down. So too with the civilization crafted into being for us by the Faith: it must be loved and defended. We might all read Belloc's meditation "Wall of the City": within, the busy commerce of decent men who go about the pots and pans of life and who worship God as he is carried through the streets in the monstrance — and without, the enemy! Belloc articulated that enemy for his own time. The enemy is the barbarian, but he always used the word analogically; and the older barbarian before the walls comes off better than his modern counterpart for Belloc. "The Barbarian" within is the man who laughs at the fixed convictions of our inheritance. He is the man with a perpetual sneer on his lips. He is above it all: he judges the poor believer in the street or in the church, some old woman huddled before a shrine of the Virgin mumbling her beads, and he judges her harshly. It is hard enough to come by belief and to live in it, but to throw it away for a cheap joke is despicable. Such are the Barbarians.

> The Barbarian hopes — and that is the mark of him, that he can have his cake and eat it too. He will consume what civilization has slowly produced after generations of selection and effort, but he will not be at pains to replace such goods, nor indeed has he a comprehension of the virtue that has brought them into being. Discipline seems to him irrational, on which account he is ever marvelling that civilization, should have offended him with priests and soldiers. . . . In a word, the Barbarian is discoverable everywhere in this, that he cannot *make:* that he can befog and destroy but that he cannot sustain; and of every Barbarian in the decline or peril of every civilization exactly that has been true.

Belloc is describing just about everyone you met at your last cocktail party or faculty meeting. Barbarians are everywhere.

Listen to Belloc again in words written from the solitude of the Sahara as he pondered the ruins of Timgad:

> We sit by and watch the Barbarian, we tolerate him; in the long stretches of peace we are not afraid. We are tickled by his irreverence, his comic inversion of our old certitudes and our fixed creeds refreshes us; we laugh. But as we laugh we are watched by large and awful faces from beyond: and on these faces there is no smile.

Of these men he added — and this too from the desert — "Their Faiths turn to legend, and at last they enter that shrine whose God has departed and whose Idol is quite blind." When our Lord vanishes from the household shrines of the West, the drums are muted and men worship abstractions — as they do today — new idols. But behind them there is an awful power, and it is not of this world.

Possessed of a highly poetic and prophetic mind, Belloc possessed as well a sharply honed intelligence. His *The Servile State* is a prolonged syllogism with not a metaphor in the whole book. His general thesis, argued in 1909, that the West was moving toward neither pure socialism nor pure capitalism is today a commonplace. It happened. We can either mourn or delight in our consumerist society. I get the impression that Belloc did a little of both. Be that as it may, his "distributist society" lies outside the scope of this paper. His *Survivals and New Arrivals* is closer to my subject. Islam, he predicted, will return because Islam is a permanent menace to the Faith. Islam has returned. Bible Christianity or Bibliolatry could return but probably will not: Belloc was wrong. Fundamentalism is with us everywhere today in the United States: vulgar, as Belloc said it always was, primitive in thought, as Belloc pointed out; sophisticated in its use of an electronic technology which he could not have predicted. Arianism, the modern name of which is modernism, has come back with a vengeance in the Church. Belloc sketched that possibility as well. All of his predictions in this interesting book were closely reasoned, but such argumentation, he admitted it, is often mocked by the mystery of the future. His reasoning prowess truly came into its own in several controversies: one with Coulton on medieval Catholicism, where Coulton got the facts right but turned the picture upside down; one with H. G. Wells on the origin of man, where Belloc complained privately that the Church hampered him because it has swallowed "all that Hebrew folklore"; and, finally, one with Dean Inge, where Belloc nails his enemy to the wall.

After answering point by point Dean Inge's objections to Catholicism — some of them were infantile: no man can be an Englishman and a Catholic; others were vicious: the Church is "a bloody and treacherous association" and an "imposter" — Belloc concluded his open letter with the following peroration. I beg your leave to read it as he wrote it:

> There wholly escapes you the character of the Catholic Church. . . .
> You are like one examining the windows of Chartres from within
> by candle-light but we have the sun shining through. . . . For
> what is the Catholic Church? It is that which replies, co-ordinates,
> establishes. It is that within which is right order; outside the
> puerilities and the despairs. It is the possession of perspective in
> the survey of the world. . . . Here alone is promise, and here alone
> is foundation. Those of us who boast so stable an endowment
> make no claim thereby to personal peace; we are not saved
> thereby alone. . . . But we are of so glorious a company that we
> receive support, and have communion. The Mother of God is
> also our own. Our dead are with us. Even in these our earthly
> miseries we always hear the distant something of an eternal music,
> and smell a native air. There is a standard set for us whereto our
> whole selves respond, which is that of an inherited and endless
> life, quite full, in our own country. You may say, "all that is
> rhetoric." You would be wrong, for it is rather vision, recogni-
> tion, and testimony. But take it for rhetoric. Have *you* any such?
> Be it but rhetoric, whence does that stream flow? Or what reserve
> is that which can fill even such a man as myself with fire? Can
> *your* opinion (or doubt or gymnastics) do the same? I think not!
> One thing in this world is different from all others. It has a per-
> sonality and a force. It is recognized and (when recognized) most
> violently hated or loved. It is the Catholic Church. Within that
> household the human spirit has roof and hearth. Outside it is
> the night.

> In haec urbe lux
>   sollennis,
> Ver aeternum, pax
>   perennis
> Et aeterna gaudia.

He once wrote that the French are blessed by the capacity to criticize themselves and to surmount their own criticism. Be that as it may, Hilaire Belloc rarely criticized the Church. He loved her altogether too much. He never answered personal attacks by fellow Catholics. It would have been, he said, a sin against his own body. Times change, and today a Catholic writer can make a good living attacking his own Mother. But Hilaire Belloc, coupled in memory always with his great friend G. K. Chesterton, made the defence of the Faith the main business of his life. He wielded a mighty sword. "Gigantes autem erant in terram in diebus illis." "There were giants upon the earth in those days" (Gen 6:4). But the sword of Hilaire Belloc was buried with him. I gravely doubt whether we shall see his like again.

ALICE VON HILDEBRAND

DIETRICH VON HILDEBRAND:
HUMAN AND PHILOSOPHICAL PROFILE

This talk does not aim primarily at expounding the rich philosophical and religious contributions that my late husband has left us. His many books and articles, and his still more numerous unpublished papers, are persuasive witnesses to his intellectual accomplishments. My aim, rather, is to try to shed light on the man whose works are so intimately related to his faith and to his personality. What I hope to accomplish is to help his readers understand better what he was trying to do, and why. Since "The Child is father of the Man", let us begin with his youth.

Son of the famous German sculptor Adolf von Hildebrand, Dietrich had the blessing of being born and raised in Florence, Italy. If ever a man had a blessed youth, that man was Dietrich von Hildebrand. The last child of loving parents, both of whom were talented and outstanding personalities, he was preceded by five sisters, who turned out to be remarkable women. They all shared with their little brother their own accomplishments in the fields of painting, sculpture, and music. One cannot imagine a more beautiful background. Surrounded by beauty from his cradle on, fed on the great cultural tradition of Europe, acquainted with the greatest works of art and with the great personalities of the day, he certainly was given, humanly speaking, what every man longs for: love and beauty. And yet, in all this beauty, joy, and warmth, something was sadly lacking: he received no religious formation whatsoever. Both of his parents were liberal Protestants in name; in fact, they were simply noble pagans.

At the age of fourteen, the young von Hildebrand took a walk with his oldest sister, Eva (nicknamed Nini), in the course of which she tried to convince him that all moral values are relative to the age and society in which a person happens to live. To the lady's amazement (she was twenty-seven at the time), the young boy vigorously opposed her views, and actually forced her into a corner by his powerful arguments. Ruffled by the earnestness of this attack in which she had so obviously been defeated, she, upon coming home, turned to their father for support, saying: "Imagine, Gogo [his nickname from his earliest youth] does not want to see that all moral values are relative." "But Nini," the father retorted, "do not forget that he is only fourteen." Piqued, the young boy answered: "Father, if you have no better argument to raise against my position than my age, then your own position must rest on a very shaky ground." At fifteen, Dietrich read several dialogues of Plato in Greek, and he fell in love with philosophy. The pursuit of truth—the capacity to distinguish truth from error, the certain from the uncertain, the evident from the doubtful—fascinated him. He was already deeply convinced, as we saw, of the objectivity of both truth and moral values. The reading of Plato's works then revealed to him his vocation: he would be a philosopher. Never, absolutely never, did he sway or hesitate about his choice. His irrevocable decision was made in spite of the opposition of his father, who did not consider philosophy to be a "serious" intellectual pursuit, much less a career, for his son.

At the age of seventeen, he became a *civis academicus* and entered the University of Munich, where he studied under Theodor Lipps. Soon afterward, he made the acquaintance of Max Scheler—this incredibly talented and rich mind who, after he made so many valuable contributions to Catholic thought, died outside the Church because he had abandoned his valid wife, Maerit Furtwaengler, in order to marry Maria Schue. For this reason, he was *ipso facto* excommunicated.

From the first moment of their acquaintance, von Hildebrand

recognized in Scheler the marks of genius. There was a man who managed to transform into gold whatever he touched. Everything became interesting, alive, fascinating. Even modest topics were magically transformed by the light of his genius. The young Dietrich, however, soon became aware of serious flaws in the thinking of Scheler, who lacked any form of discipline, whether intellectual or moral. Nevertheless, he was to remain deeply indebted to Scheler for the rest of his life. Not only did Scheler "inspire" him and open new horizons to him, but, most important of all, Scheler was the very first person who revealed to him the reality of the supernatural.

To repeat: von Hildebrand was born and raised in an ideal background; he was given whatever a noble pagan can wish for: talent, affection, joy, beauty, a secure life. But even though he had been born and raised in Italy, he was totally ignorant of Roman Catholicism. He appreciated Christian art exclusively for its beauty, overlooking its deep symbolism and spiritual message.

But thanks to Scheler—a fallen-away Catholic, living in sin—he discovered a new world, a world of supernatural beauty, which infinitely transcended what natural beauty could possibly offer. This discovery, which was to revolutionize his life, came to him when Scheler (who repeatedly declared himself to be a sinner) spoke to him about the Catholic saints. A saint? Sanctity? These questions were answered by Scheler, who sketched in vibrant terms the phenomenon of saintliness. He spoke to the young man about Saint Francis of Assisi. The discovery of the *Poverello* was to be decisive in Dietrich's religious development.

Scheler had planted a seed that would blossom fully some seven years later, when, on Holy Saturday 1914, Dietrich and his wife, Margaret Denk, entered the Roman Catholic Church. They had been preceded in this by one of his sisters and would be followed by the other four.

In his book *Surprised by Joy*, C. S. Lewis tells us that when he had found his way back to God, he was the most despondent convert in the whole of England. The situation was exactly the reverse in von Hildebrand's case: he was the most radiant convert in Germany—nay, in any country. For him, the discovery of the supernatural was inebriating. The natural world, however, lost none of its charm and beauty, although it paled in comparison to the glorious beauty that he had discovered through faith. Inebriated by this revelation, the young convert was filled with a holy enthusiasm.

He was conscious of his intellectual gifts, and he had, as I have said, a passionate love for philosophy, which never waned. He once told me, "When I can no longer philosophize, call a priest; the end is near." But however great and noble and fascinating philosophy was, it could not match the new world opened up to him by revelation. Infinitely more beautiful, its radiance was unique. The delights that revelation afforded him transcended whatever intellectual joys he had experienced in his long exchanges with Scheler when, at a Munich café, the two would sometimes spend the night in spirited philosophical discussions.

The following account will illumine this point. When he started taking instructions in the Faith, von Hildebrand was greatly surprised to learn the Roman Catholic teaching that artificial contraception is sinful. This teaching baffled him. What could possibly be wrong about preventing a life from coming into existence? He was keenly conscious of the fact that he had a strong ethical sense; how, then, could he have failed to perceive that artificial birth control is morally wrong? But the priest who instructed him was adamant: "If you want to become a Roman Catholic, you must accept the totality of Catholic teaching in both faith and morals. You cannot pick and choose. Total adherence to the Church's teaching is a *conditio sine qua non* for your being accepted into the Church." Without a moment's hesitation, the young man said: "*Credo ut intelligam*. The Church has spoken, I want to submit to her teaching, and whether I understand it or not is irrelevant. This is God's word." Soon afterward, he was granted such deep insights into the immoral-

ity of artificial contraception that he became one of the greatest
Catholic champions of the Church's position. In the early 1930s,
he wrote an article pointing to the ambiguities of the so-called
Lambeth Declaration, whereby "cautious approval" was given
to contraceptive practices of married couples. And in 1968,
when Pope Paul VI published *Humanae Vitae,* von Hildebrand
was the very first Catholic thinker to take up the defense of
this embattled encyclical. His small book *Humanae Vitae: A Sign
of Contradiction* was published in September of 1968.

Submission to the teaching of the Church on the part of a
young man so outstandingly talented is deeply significant. Convinced as he was of the objectivity of truth, and of man's intellectual capacity to reach it, he was also convinced that man's
intellectual powers had been affected by original sin and that
the Church's infallible teaching is a gift of incomparable value
to the philosopher. If ever there was a man who appreciated
the fecundating value of faith for human reason, that man was
Dietrich von Hildebrand. His profound faith assured him that
there could be no conflict between faith and reason. When the
Church spoke in matters of faith and morals, faithful Catholics
had simply to say: "Roma locuta est; causa finita est." It was
as simple as that. Submission to the Church's teaching cost him
no effort. On the contrary, he experienced the deep joy of hum-
bling his mind before his Creator. Having entered with joy and
fervent conviction into the Roman Catholic Church, he wanted
to put his talents at her disposal: to receive and understand and
explain Church teaching, not to contest and distort it.

When, shortly before his death, he solemnly confided his intellectual legacy to me, he said: "If ever you discover in my
work a thought which is not in complete harmony with the
teaching of Holy Church, do not hesitate for a moment to de-
stroy the manuscript." How many Catholic intellectuals, especially today, are ever moved to utter such words?

It has often been contended that to become a Roman Catholic means to agree to denigrate reason, to abandon academic
excellence, and to become an intellectual slave. Secular univer-

sities (as I can testify) abound with people who consider that
any serious religious affiliation, particularly Catholic affiliations,
actually paralyzes a person's mind, imprisoning him in the
straightjacket of arbitrary dogmas which defy reason and ob-
struct any free intellectual pursuit. They are deeply convinced
that adherence to the dogmatic teaching of the Church deprives
a man of his "freedom of thought" and reduces him to the level
of an intellectual parrot. A case in point is Husserl's reaction
to von Hildebrand's conversion in 1914. "Alas," Husserl said,
"a great talent has been lost to philosophy; he has become a
Roman Catholic." When von Hildebrand's doctoral disserta-
tion was to be published in the famous *Journal for Phenomeno-
logical Research,* the young author made a few minor corrections
and additions. For an example of a moral action resplendent
with the beauty of something intrinsically good in and by itself, he pointed to the attitude of Saint Steven, the first martyr, toward his murderers. Husserl, reviewing the galleys,
wrote in the margin, "Roman Catholic propaganda".

After converting to Roman Catholicism, von Hildebrand felt
called to be a confessor. That is to say, he would not shyly hide
his faith and make people believe that nothing important had
happened to him. What had happened to him was so overwhelming, so revolutionary, that he wanted it to penetrate into
every fiber of his being, and his life. He wanted people to know
that—however much he loved philosophy, art, music, and nature, all great natural values—he had now discovered a higher
reality, the reality of the supernatural. From now on, he always considered the primary aim of his life to be the glorification of God as achieved by man's "Transformation in Christ".
To quote the great Cardinal Newman, with whom he had so
much intellectual and religious affinity, "Holiness rather than
peace". Von Hildebrand strove for holiness as long as he lived;
he was not to know much exterior peace.

It would, however, be completely wrong to believe that he
lost interest in philosophy. His passion for philosophical questions stayed with him throughout his long life. Philosophy was

in the very marrow of his bones. But he had discovered a greater love, and it was no longer conceivable that philosophy should play first fiddle in his intellectual life. From now on, his faith was first and foremost. His *Memoirs* include a deeply revealing sentence to the effect that the young man who had always had a passion for the ethical had now discovered something much higher: the supernatural morality resplendent in the lives of the saints. This "new" morality actually was a perfect fulfillment of natural morality. For this reason, like Kierkegaard before him, von Hildebrand always considered Christian morality to be not one possible morality among others but the one true morality, valid for all people. Natural virtues such as modesty, truthfulness, generosity, and courage are, indeed, beautiful and noble, and the great pagans have rightly praised them. But they have been superseded by supernatural virtues, such as humility and charity. Their being superseded, however, in no way means that they lose their importance and validity. On the contrary, they shine with an even brighter light. But they are now seen in their subordination to the higher Christian virtues of humility and charity, the perfume of which had inebriated von Hildebrand when he read the life of Francis of Assisi.

Even though the religious sphere had become the beacon of his life after his conversion, he refrained from writing anything religious for several years. Conscious that he needed to learn, he became completely receptive. For years, he spent every free moment at the Library of Munich, to deepen his knowledge of his newly acquired faith. He read the history of the Church, the writings of the Fathers and the Doctors of the Church, the history of the foundation of religious orders, and the lives of the saints. In the course of several years of this holy fare, he accumulated a formidable treasure of Catholic spirituality, which was to fecundate and inspire his mind and his writings for the rest of his life.

After seven years of complete receptivity, he felt that the moment had come for him to take his pen in hand and share with others what he himself had received. The very first article he wrote after his conversion, entitled "The New World of Christianity", was dedicated to the special quality of "holiness" typical of the supernatural world, holiness made visible in the Sacred Humanity of Christ, the Epiphany of God. In this article, he tried to show the completely new quality of the supernatural Christian ethos in contrast to all purely natural values. This theme ran through the whole remainder of my late husband's life and found its most perfect expression in his religious masterpiece, *Transformation in Christ*. In this first article, he expressed great joy over his conversion. But simultaneously, with a sort of prophetic insight, he warned against the increasing menace of secularization within the Catholic Church, particularly within university circles. He remarked with sorrow that professors enjoyed more recognition than priests, even though the latter acquired through their ordination an extraordinary dignity that no professor could ever hope to attain on the natural level. He also lamented that scholarship was more highly prized than faith.

When he worked on his *Habilitation,* his mentor, the respected Professor Baeumker (a Catholic), advised him that within the university precincts he should carefully abstain from using the word *religion.* "Young man," he said, "replace 'religion' with 'metaphysics'; it sounds more respectable." Such advice von Hildebrand did not follow then or at any later period. Professor Baeumker was a good man, a faithful Catholic. He wanted simply to protect a young, inexperienced thinker from making blunders that would jeopardize his career. But the young convert was aghast. How could someone born in the Faith, nurtured from his youth on this precious nectar, feel shy about revealing to others the gift that he had received? God exists; Christ, the Second Person of the Holy Trinity, became man, suffered and died on the Cross in order to save humanity. Were these overwhelming realities to be put in brackets as soon as one entered a university? It struck him as incomprehensible, very much as if people wanted to put the sun into brackets.

Let me emphasize that von Hildebrand never confused faith with reason. He knew full well that philosophical work is based exclusively on reason, as opposed to theology, which presupposes an acceptance of revelation. In his teaching, he never used his faith as an argument to defend or buttress a philosophical position. But neither did he hesitate to show the harmony existing between the content of faith and the philosophical conclusions which he had reached.

Baeumker — like very many German professors — considered the university to be sacred ground, having its own rules, rules that should be respected as soon as one stepped into its boundaries. These rules decreed that research, scholarship, and pure reason were supreme and absolute and that everything else was to be banned. For von Hildebrand, however, a university was indeed respectable, but he certainly refused to absolutize its value. He knew full well that, although universities have played a tremendous role in the intellectual and cultural formation of Europe, they have, at times, also nurtured thinkers whose ideas were poisonous, because false, and who were responsible for innumerable evils which have harmed the world. I do not recall whether my late husband had read Chesterton's *The Man Who Was Thursday,* but I am convinced that he would have loved the following passage: "The dangerous criminal is the educated criminal. We say that the most dangerous criminal now is the entirely lawless modern philosopher. Compared to him, burglars and bigamists are essentially moral men; my heart goes out to them."

Atheism, relativism, subjectivism, idealism, Marxism, Freudianism, etc., were all born in the academy and were all spread by intellectuals. When a university endorses the famous words of Socrates: "I am interested in nothing but the truth" (*Euthyphro*), it is a marvelous place. But to the extent that it "welcomes all ideas" (Mother Elizabeth McCormack in her inaugural speech as president of Manhattanville College), without distinguishing the wheat from the dross, truth from error, the fashionable from the intrinsically valid, the good from the evil, a university can become a dangerous fortress ensconcing error, a nursery of false philosophies. Von Hildebrand was soon to see how the deification of universities had corrupted many of its members, for he was to witness with sorrow the positive stand that most German professors took toward Nazism. Their blindness and cowardice toward Hitler's doctrine were the inevitable result of their attitude toward life in general and the university in particular.

When von Hildebrand started teaching at the University of Munich, he had several students who were young priests. Because they had received the sacrament of ordination, he always made a point of treating them with special respect; he would let them pass through the door ahead of him. This did not remain unnoticed by his colleagues. One day, one of them called him aside and said to him, "Why do you let your students step ahead of you? You seem to forget that you are a Herr Professor." "In no way do I forget it," von Hildebrand answered, "but I mean to pay tribute to the extraordinary dignity which priests have received." "But", the irate professor retorted, "they are only students, and in so doing you offend against the dignity of your rank." Von Hildebrand answered: "You forget that their hands hold the body of our Lord; this fact explains my behavior." His colleague looked at him despisingly. Here was a young professor who seemed incapable of understanding the importance of university professors and the role that they played in German society. Von Hildebrand's behavior was thus a threat to their professorial dignity.

After he had published *In Defense of Purity* (a book that was to be translated into five languages), he was one day called aside by one of his most amiable fellow professors, who said: "Dear Herr Colleague, may I give you some friendly advice? I notice that you have published a book about purity. As a friend truly caring about your welfare, I advise you to refrain from writing on topics which belong to a young girls' boarding school. Why don't you write on Siger of Brabant? Little work has been done on this thinker. If you write on him, you will increase enormously your chances of ascending in the hierarchy of the university." After thanking him for his kind advice, von Hildebrand retorted: "You see, I happen to believe that purity is a virtue of crucial importance in human life, but I have little interest in Siger of Brabant." His friendly colleague looked at him with a mixture of amazement and pity. How could someone be so stupid as not to understand that purity is not very highly valued among professors!

Von Hildebrand was much encouraged, however, by the receipt of a personal letter of congratulations from Monsignor Pacelli, who was nuncio in Germany at the time. He conveyed his judgment that the book on purity was magnificent. Von Hildebrand valued the praise of this remarkable Catholic dignitary more highly than the approval of the whole university senate. Even so, this new young professor was not making himself very popular among his colleagues. He did, however, enjoy great popularity among the students, who were amazed that a professor would condescend to talk to them and even joke with them. As one of them put it, "He is the friendliest of professors."

But the religious question was not the only one that would make von Hildebrand unpopular at the University of Munich and jeopardize his chances of "reaching the top of the scale". There was also the question of German militarism and nationalism. Prior to his conversion, he was vigorously opposed to both. This opposition, therefore, did not spring from his faith, but it was reinforced by it. The essence of nationalism is a deification of one's country, nurtured on the principle "My country, right or wrong." Militarism is the glorification of brutal force. Both principles are basically anti-Christian. God alone has a right to our complete and absolute allegiance, and the Christian way is one of conquering love, not brutality and violence.

Even prior to his *Habilitation* in 1918, von Hildebrand discovered that German university professors were violently nationalistic and militaristic. A case in point is the treatment meted out to Friedrich Wilhelm Foerster, the great enemy of militaristic Prussia. Professor at the University of Munich, he had taken a year's leave of absence. Upon his return in 1916, he gave a talk severely criticizing German militarism as well as the German atrocities committed in Belgium during the occupation. Foerster was immediately labeled a traitor. When he was about to resume teaching at the university, a protest demonstration was staged against him. Von Hildebrand was working on his *Habilitation* at the time. His mentor, Professor Baeumker, begged him to keep a low profile. Von Hildebrand acquiesced. But when Foerster made his appearance and was greeted with catcalls and insults, von Hildebrand forgot all about his promise to Baeumker. Using his powerful lungs, he started a counter-chant: "Hoch Foerster!" (Long live Foerster!) His leadership and the strength of his personality were such that the tide was quickly turned, and the affair ended with a complete victory for the courageous German pedagogue. We may well appreciate how troubled Professor Baeumker was about his young protégé, who had turned out to be an *enfant terrible*. This experience was an eye-opener to von Hildebrand. He understood that masses were blind forces that could be manipulated and drawn toward good or evil, according to the leader influencing them.

Then came the defeat of 1918. This was a terrible blow to German militaristic pride and brought in its wake a catastrophic economic situation. No doubt life was extremely difficult in defeated Germany, and the political unrest was great. One murder followed another, and the stage was being prepared for the rise of Nazism, which promised to restore Germany to its "God-given role" as political, military, and cultural leader of the world. As a matter of fact, the despairing German people were repeatedly told by Nazi propaganda that they were the greatest race in the world, the master race. What a balm that was on the festering wound of their nationalistic pride! Let us not forget that Max Scheler, who had been expelled from the University of Munich after a sex scandal, had written a book during the war, praising Germany and her great cultural mis-

sion, a book which was to guarantee his prestige and success
for the rest of his life. For this book was received enthusiasti-
cally by the German people; and all of a sudden, all the nasty
rumors about Scheler's private life were forgotten, and he became a German intellectual hero.

Not so von Hildebrand. Attending a pacifist congress in Paris
in 1921, he declared that the German invasion of Belgium on
August 4, 1914, was "un crime atroce". He said so because he
thought so, and he thought so because it was true. The inviol-
ability of Belgian soil had been guaranteed by a treaty of neu-
trality signed in the name of the Holy Trinity by five nations.
But the Germans broke their solemn commitment. They reasoned that "Not kennt kein Gebot" (Necessity knows no law)
and invaded Belgian territory, where they gave free vent to
their Teutonic fury.

Upon coming back to Munich, von Hildebrand found his
wife, Gretchen, distraught. Some reporter had written an article distorting the words and the meaning of von Hildebrand's
intervention. The reporter claimed that the young professor
had declared Germany and Germany alone to be responsible
for the war. Von Hildebrand in no way had held or expressed
this position. Having no access to secret documents and files,
he felt incompetent to pass judgment on this thorny issue. He
did, however, say that if history proved Germany to be guilty,
he would have no difficulty in acknowledging the fact. Truth
to him was more important than nationalism.

He also found a letter from the senate of the University of
Munich stating that he would be expelled from the university
if he could not clear himself of the charges made against him.
He managed to weather the storm, but the nascent Nazi movement carefully noted the name of this "traitor", promising themselves that they would take care of him when their hour had
come. This is why on November 8, 1923, when Hitler launched
his famous putsch in Munich, von Hildebrand's name was on
the blacklist, and he had to escape to Württemberg. Had he
been caught, he would have been shot within an hour, after

a show trial. Hitler was promptly defeated this time, but the
Nazis and their allies among university professors became convinced that von Hildebrand was a traitor who had to be closely
watched.

No one will be surprised to learn that he did not "ascend in
the hierarchy" of the university. He had now firmly established
his reputation of being both a fanatical Catholic and a political
traitor. These two accusations would stand in his way throughout his career in Germany and in Austria.

In a rare case of failing to estimate a situation accurately, von
Hildebrand had erroneously assumed in 1923 that Nazism was
dead. A few years later, however, he became alarmed by the
increasing political unrest in Germany and by the eruption of
an increasingly virulent nationalism. He realized that the Nazi
danger was still lurking underground. The good forces were
(as usual) fast asleep, and the evil forces were working day and
night to achieve their aim: the conquest of Germany. In the
late 1920s, he realized, to his sorrow, that some basic tenets of
Nazi philosophy had deeply penetrated into the German consciousness. The slogan *Boden und Blut* (Soil and Blood) appeared
more and more often in different places. In intellectual circles,
collectivism was gaining ground at a fearful pace.

To meet such dangers head on, von Hildebrand began writing one of his major works, *Metaphysics of Community*. Unfortunately totally unknown in this country, this is a book of
crucial importance. In it he shows the supremacy that the individual person should possess over the collective, for the person alone has an immortal soul. He blasts collectivism, basic
to both Nazism and Communism, which idolizes the state and
sees man as having the function of a cog in a wheel. He develops a theory of the hierarchy of communities, with the Holy
Church at the very top.

But the evil was spreading like fire. When Hitler gained control of the German state in January 1933, von Hildebrand saw
clearly that he had but two alternatives. On the one hand, he
could remain in Germany, witness all the horrors and injustices

which he knew would be committed, keep a low profile, and
muzzle his conscience; or, on the other hand, he would have
to leave the country. As a professor of ethics, and as a Catholic, he knew it was his duty to raise his voice against evil. He
also knew that, were he to do so, he would end in a concen-
tration camp within hours. At the age of forty-three, therefore, he embraced the second alternative. He left Germany and
found himself a beggar, without a home, without a position,
cut off from his dearest friends. He went to Florence, where
his sister Elizabeth Brewster was living in the house in which
he was born, and she generously gave him hospitality. But
when he realized that the Austrian chancellor Dollfuss was putting up a courageous fight against Nazism, he went to Vienna
and offered his intellectual services. With Dollfuss' help, he
founded an anti-Nazi, antitotalitarian magazine, *Der christliche
Staendestaat,* to which he devoted all his energies. Apart from
his courses at the University of Vienna, which he began to offer
in January 1935 (in spite of violent Nazi demonstrations against
his appointment), he devoted all his time to fighting against
the evil of Nazism. He totally gave up strictly philosophical
work, on the principle that, when the house is burning, one
must give priority to extinguishing the conflagration. He was
no ivory-tower philosopher.

The years in Vienna were years of trial. He soon discovered
that on many issues he was fearfully alone. Even worse, after
Dollfuss' assassination on July 25, 1934, he found himself *per-
sona non grata* with the Schuschnigg government. Schuschnigg
was in no way a Nazi, but neither was he a sharp-sighted poli-
tician. He wanted to achieve "peaceful coexistence" with "our
brothers, the Germans". His naive attitude had severe personal
consequences for von Hildebrand. First, Schuschnigg cut off the
funds which Dollfuss had pledged for the publication of the
magazine; moreover, yielding to political pressures, Schuschnigg did not grant von Hildebrand the professorship promised
him by Dollfuss. He gave him instead a position of lower rank,
with a minimial salary.

When the time came for von Hildebrand to teach, opposition to his appointment was such that a demonstration was organized to prevent him from giving his *Antrittsvorlesung.* Students armed with clubs and sticks crowded into the auditorium where he was to give his first lecture. The police had to be called. Escorted by forty-eight heavily armed policemen, he finally managed to give his talk. He found out later that the protesting students had been encouraged by their professors to intimidate him—an unwelcome new member of the faculty.

Then, in January 1935, he was warned by the chief of police that the Gestapo underground was planning to assassinate him. For thirty-nine months, he had to live under the sword of Damocles.

That his work was successful cannot be denied. I have a copy of a "top secret" letter that the German ambassador to Vienna, Franz von Papen, wrote to Hitler, warning him that von Hildebrand was the worst obstacle to what he was trying to accomplish in Austria. Moreover, after the war Schuschnigg revealed that in his famous meeting with Adolf Hitler in Berchtesgaden on February 12, 1938—during which Hitler outlined his conditions for not invading Austria—one of the conditions was that the Austrian chancellor must curb the journalistic activities of von Hildebrand. Then, when Hitler did invade Austria on March 11, 1938, my late husband's name headed the list of nongovernmental people to be arrested immediately.

On the very day of the *Anschluss,* he miraculously escaped, thanks to a Swiss passport—a precious gift he had inherited from his grandfather, Bruno Hildebrand. Himself condemned to death in 1848, Bruno had escaped to Switzerland, where he was granted an honorary citizenship in gratitude for his service to the Swiss state.

My husband spent eleven months in Switzerland, living off the incredible generosity of Swiss Catholics. He was then appointed professor at the Catholic University of Toulouse in France. But soon the Nazi barbarians invaded France, and he had to go into hiding to escape the ever-widening grasp of the

DIETRICH VON HILDEBRAND   113

Gestapo. Once again, he was miraculously saved, this time thanks to the heroism of French Catholics, especially Edmond Michelet, who later became minister of the army under de Gaulle.

He arrived in the United States just before Christmas in 1940. Here he resumed his professional work, but under extremely unpropitious conditions. His wife was ailing. His son had three small children but no job. Von Hildebrand could never afford a secretary. He depended instead upon the goodwill of friends. Once I had completed my doctorate, I volunteered to type his manuscripts in what time remained after my own teaching responsibilities at Hunter College. His productivity increased wonderfully. He made up for all the years of philosophical inactivity forced upon him by the political situation.

To return now to my main theme: What was von Hildebrand's attitude toward life and toward philosophy? A passage in Cardinal Newman's *Apologia* recently caught my attention: "The truth is, I was beginning to prefer intellectual excellence to moral; I was drifting in the direction of liberalism." May I note that, intellectually and religiously speaking, there is more than one analogy between my late husband and the great English cardinal, for whom, by the way, he entertained the greatest admiration. But whereas the young John Henry Newman was tempted, as he admits above, to put intellectual values above moral values, such a temptation was completely alien to von Hildebrand. I have never met an intellectual less tempted to do this than he. Just as some persons receive the grace of never being tempted by impurity, so he was never tempted to place the intellectual above the moral. This immunity was certainly not due to any failure to appreciate intellectual values, which played a crucial role in his life. But from his youth on, he was acutely conscious of the unique role that moral values are called upon to play in man's life. Moral values reigned supreme in his estimate until the time of his conversion, when they yielded to the religion of Christ, which embraces and completes genuine morality.

As much as he loved his work and was happy in his profession, anyone could interrupt him at any time. He would gladly have given up the writing of a book for the sake of helping someone into the Church. How many hours did he sacrifice counseling those in difficult love and marriage situations? In his *Memoirs* he even mentions that he once took a night train to Rome in order to speak to a young man who could not make up his mind about a girl he loved. Von Hildebrand spent one day talking to the young man and then took another night train back to Munich, to arrive on time for his course at the university.

Two thoughts crucial to his ethical work also characterized his everyday life. The first is what he calls "the spirit of response to value". There are objective values in the world, "precious and good and beautiful things", which call for a response on our part proportionate to their rank and quality. The second is the fact that values occupy a clear-cut hierarchy. Some are higher, some are lower; and, *ceteris paribus,* the higher must be given precedence over the lower.

How easy it was for him to praise those who truly deserved praise! How spontaneous and warmhearted his praise was! He judged a work by its own merit. He could be enthusiastic about the accomplishments of others, even though the colleague praised might show little understanding or appreciation for his own work. Von Hildebrand never feared that his praise of others might somehow diminish his own merit or his own accomplishments. When the theme was to evaluate another person's work, he did so with intelligent fairness. One need only read his *Memoirs* to see how often and how warmly he praises the work of others, and how he rejoices to meet a truly great mind, such as Scheler, Reinach, Husserl, and to a certain extent Foerster; and, of course, the great minds of the past, which nourished his own mind and his own heart. But for von Hildebrand, the praise of both the dead and the living came with equal ease, as long as they objectively deserved praise.

There is another facet of his personality that I would like to mention briefly—namely, his exceptional understanding for what I would like to call "the mystery of femininity". I am profoundly convinced that, however hateful radical feminism seems today, it would never have developed into the poisonous blossoms to be found in some of the most famous feminists if there had been more men like Dietrich von Hildebrand. Some women have become feminists no doubt solely because they react with bitterness to their unjust treatment at the hands of some men. Too many men, but by no means all, have a macho complex. They assume as a matter of course that they are superior beings because they are males. Some of them, moreover, are brutally selfish. By contrast, my late husband had an extraordinarily fine understanding for the values incarnated in the female sex. Already as a little boy, he had asked his mother why women were so much more attractive than men. When he was nine years old, he even wrote a drama to praise the female sex. His play ended with a very typical remark: "In general, women are superior to men; but in one respect men are superior, for they love women, who deserve it more, whereas women love men." The spirit of "response to value" was already fully alive in this unusual child.

Because of his special understanding for the mystery of femininity, he had a talent for opening a woman's eyes to the greatness and beauty of her mission, as virgin, wife, mother, or simply as woman. He told me many times that, in the course of his long life, he had met more extraordinary women than extraordinary men. Obviously, he knew more men than women who were "creative" in the fields of theology, philosophy, science, technology, architecture, the arts. But to his mind, a person's "being" was more important than exterior accomplishments. Whether because women tend to be more religious than men (the very weakness of their condition gives them a keener sense of their creatureliness); or because they are better able to sustain genuine receptivity, which is essential to holiness; or because their very body is often a burden that helps them understand the mystery and fruitfulness of suffering lovingly accepted, it is a fact that in many cases women are religiously and morally superior to men. One particularly horrible facet of feminism consists precisely in the infamous tradeoff desired by radical feminists. They wish to sell this real moral and religious superiority for a mess of pottage: fame, power, money. My husband's special understanding for the mystery of femininity sheds light on one crucial principle of his philosophy: the truth that man can transcend himself. It is simply wrong to claim with Simone de Beauvoir that a man cannot truly understand a woman because he belongs to the opposite sex. It is precisely because he is a man that he is given a key to understanding the woman he loves. My husband was convinced that no man can possibly understand another man as deeply as a woman who loves him can, just as no woman can understand another woman as deeply as a loving man can.

Not only did he have a profound understanding of the mystery of femininity, but he also usually preferred to talk to women rather than to men. This should not be interpreted to mean that he did not fully appreciate contact with men who were either noble personalities or talented thinkers or artists. His life was enriched by many beautiful male friendships, particularly with his *alter ego,* Siegfried Johannes Hamburger. But he enjoyed talking to women because they approached problems and ideas from another angle and because he knew that God had meant men and women to be complementary—so that a talk with a loving or intelligent woman had a fecundating influence on the male mind. Moreover, he found women to be more receptive; their minds were less cluttered by theories and abstractions. The fact that many of them were not scholars impressed him as a blessing, for he had an intense dislike of dry, pedantic scholarship. Even prior to his conversion, his attitude toward women was pervaded by a deep reverence. He states in his *Memoirs* that he could never have had a friendship with any man who looked down on women or considered them to be objects of pleasure. Men like this filled him with horror and disgust. His own reverent "prephilosophical" attitude toward women was no doubt the fertile soil on which blossomed his sublime thoughts on love and marriage. Centered as he was on eternity, he also was fully conscious of the fact that all the great and magnificent male accomplishments (such as artistic creation and intellectual contributions) would one day perish. But human beings, to whom women give birth in pain and travail, have immortal souls and will continue to live forever.

Von Hildebrand died almost thirteen years ago, but his thought is more alive now than ever. As a result of his writings, many people have found their way to the Church, and very many of my dear students (they must number about 10,000 strong) have benefited from the spiritual and intellectual treasures that he has so abundantly given us.

I am deeply convinced that von Hildebrand's influence will grow in the future, for no great things are time bound. Like vigorous vines, they continue to spread and to bear ever more abundant fruit. My friend John Barger of the Sophia Institute Press expends all his time and energy in reprinting some of my late husband's works, thus ensuring their increasing influence. In the short one hundred years that have passed since the birth of Dietrich von Hildebrand, we find that his thought is gloriously alive, that the truths about which he sang so ardently while on earth continue now to sound and to call forth echoes of eternity.

WILLIAM A. MARRA

VON HILDEBRAND ON LOVE, HAPPINESS, AND SEX

I should like to discuss first the link between love and that ingredient of happiness which deserves the name *joy*. Granted that happiness, to be full or perfect, demands several other perfections; but joy has to be central. Without joy, without the leaping delight of the spirit, what could happiness possibly mean?

The joys of life, whether modest or gigantic, are for the most part clearly due to our loving relations with other persons. These include the love of a parent for a child, a child for a parent, a friend for a friend, and, above all, the "spousal" or "romantic" love between two persons of opposite sex.

Our loving relation to God is by far the most important of all possible loves. But in what follows, I wish to restrict myself to our loves for human persons. I think that we need to develop accurate categories concerning the things of experience before we attempt an analysis of metaphysical realities.

In a typical human life, love comes mixed with many other things: anxiety, concern, sorrow, sacrifice. But every love also affords delight, joy. Even to know that the loved one exists, to be in her presence, to speak tender words together, to do things and enjoy things with a person we love: this is the stuff of a happy life. This brings sunshine and joy into what is usually a gray and prosaic day.

If there is no loved one in my life—no dear friend or child or parent or spouse—just what can rejoice me? Some superficial sources are no doubt available. There are gourmet meals, for example, and chances for fame (if only as a guest on some big TV show). Possessing money is not painful either, if we prescind from the hard work that often accompanies the acquiring and (perhaps even more) safeguarding it.

And there are other sources of joy which are not superficial. I think here of our commerce with beautiful things in nature and in art. These touch us, warm us, delight us, bring us to our depth. But they leave us essentially lonely in precisely the degree that we have no beloved person with whom we can share the experience.

So, too, "professional" pursuits may yield their own special kind of satisfaction and happiness. But they, too, are essentially lonely. Certain practitioners of the "intellectual life" seek to persuade at least themselves that they enjoy "a higher happiness" for the reason that their minds are fully active. They may hear the joyful laughter or heartfelt song of loving persons and dismiss the scene as one of "sense happiness", in contrast to their lofty "intellectual happiness". But they deceive themselves. Keeping the mind active, as such, may certainly bring its own kind of delight; but this is not to be compared with the music and sunshine that surround loving hearts.

Von Hildebrand took seriously the crucial distinction made by Edmund Husserl, his teacher at the University of Goettingen, between "intentional" and "non-intentional" experiences, including most emphatically those experiences called "feelings". If someone strokes my skin, or if some chemical or mechanical agent acts on some part of my body, I shall experience "feelings" — pleasant or not, welcome or not. These are the caused, nonintentional feelings. But if I respond with joy to the presence of a loved one, or with sorrow to news that a beloved person has died, or with gratitude to someone's generosity toward me — these "feelings" are in no way "bodily" — as if they arise from some agent's contact with nerve endings of my body.

On the contrary, these belong to the new, spiritual world of "intentionality" — where the person has an enlightened "rational" contact with being. That I know or understand something is thus an intentional experience; so, too, that I accomplish an inner act of willing. And so, too, are all the "feelings" that cannot even exist unless I first grasp the object. Von Hildebrand, above all in his book *The Heart* but also in many other books, at last does justice to the nature of "spiritual feelings". The traditional philosophy usually assigned the "spiritual part" to "the will" and "feeling" to the body. Under these categories, it would follow that purely bodiless persons, such as angels, would feel nothing. Their joy or love or grateful praise would somehow amount to an intellectual "volition", sharply distinguished from any "emotions" (which are supposed to be "motions" of the body).

One of von Hildebrand's greatest contributions to the philosophy of the person is his analysis of "value response". Love is such a response. For love to exist, I must grasp the beloved person as lovable, as glowing with a preciousness that already belongs to her, independent of any needs or desires of mine. I grasp that the loved one is a "value"—something "good" in herself. I discover this value, respond to it, am grateful for the encounter.

Never do I "glare" at the loved one as if to inquire how she can somehow satisfy my needs or urges or desires. This indeed happens in all those encounters precisely the opposite of value responses. Centering on myself, I regard the world as holding beings which can become "means" to my pleasures and comforts—to my "happiness" in the egotistical sense. Two radically different kinds of "good" must be distinguished here: the "value" good and what von Hildebrand terms the "subjectively satisfying" good. The latter includes all the glittering qualities that shine forth from a being just because it is able to enhance my pleasure or comfort or flatter my pride and concupiscence.

Hence, von Hildebrand is not especially impressed by the principle, enunciated as far back as Aristotle, that "man always wills the good and always desires the good." "Which good?" von Hildebrand would ask. "The good of value or the subjec-

tively satisfying good?" Nor would he agree that this distinction is equivalent to that between "the real good" and "the
apparent good", as if all our choosing of the latter kind results
from some sort of intellectual failure—some "mistake".

The joy that comes from a loving relation to another person
arises from our value response to that person. Just the fact of
her preciousness and lovability is what stirs within us love and
gratitude and delight. Yet not one of these "responses" can be
willed. I do not love the other as a "means" to a desired end—
my happiness. Rather, I approach the other for her own sake;
I am drawn toward her by her lovability. I forget myself and
all my needs and desires. And—blessed paradox of life and the
Gospels!—I am "surprised by joy". I had "surrendered" to the
precious one, loved her because she is lovable. I had forgotten
my self and my needs. I did not begin to love "in order to be
happy". Rather, my love is a response to the lovable person
who has come into my life. Joy—and laughter and sunshine—
are the "fruits" of the value response, but never the "intended
ends".

Dietrich von Hildebrand was thirty-four years old when in
1923 he gave a lecture on marriage in Ulm, Germany, at a congress of the Catholic Academic Association. Two years later,
in Innsbruck, Austria, he gave several lectures at a session of
the Federation of Catholic Students' Unions. These had to do
with "Purity and Virginity". They were published in German
under that title. The Ulm lecture appeared in a little book entitled *Marriage*. It had the enthusiastic approval of then Cardinal
Eugenio Pacelli, papal nuncio in Munich, who later became
Pope Pius XII. Translated into English during World War II,
the book enjoyed great popularity, remaining in print through
four editions over fourteen years. Out of print afterward for
almost thirty years, it has finally been republished—by Sophia
Institute Press.

The Innsbruck lectures were published in English in 1930,
but under the somewhat apologetic title *In Defense of Purity*.
This has been von Hildebrand's most popular book, having

been translated into many European languages. Simply stated, the book is a masterpiece, an original and profound study of the mystery of human sexuality and its exact relation to purity, to love, to marriage, and, above all, to consecrated virginity. For my purposes here, it suffices that I sum up the first part of the book, having to do with sex as distinguished from all other bodily "systems".

Von Hildebrand notes that, in contrast with all other bodily experiences, sex alone is essentially deep:

> Every manifestation of sex produces an effect which transcends the physical sphere and, in a fashion quite unlike the other bodily desires, involves the soul deeply in its passion. . . . The positive and negative values attaching to sex belong to a level far deeper than those which attach to the other bodily appetites.
>
> . . . The unique profundity of sex in the physical sphere is sufficiently shown by the simple fact that a man's attitude towards it is of incomparably greater moral significance than his attitude towards other bodily appetites. Surrender to sexual desire for its own sake defiles a man in a way that gluttony, for example, can never do. It wounds him to the core of his being, and he becomes in an absolutely different and novel fashion guilty of sin. . . . Sex can indeed keep silence, but when it speaks it is no mere *obiter dictum,* but a voice from the depths, the utterance of something central and of the utmost significance. In and with sex, man, in a special sense, gives himself.[1]

Scattered throughout von Hildebrand's works are many references to the great errors that always abound concerning the human person. One such error has been dealt with briefly above—namely, that which sees all human responses, and therefore love, as "means" to self-gratification. There is then the more modern error, especially egregious since Freud, which interprets all "love" as being rooted in sex drives, whether explicitly or not. This latter error becomes at least plausible when "spousal" love is at stake. For such a love occurs between the sexes and certainly is linked to sexual union in a dramatic way. How natural, then, to say that love is but a sexual drive in the first place or at least to say that on the best analysis love is but "a spiritual friendship between two persons", with sex merely superadded. Von Hildebrand rejects such interpretations of spousal love. He stresses that, in its very quality as a "spiritual" (thus, intentional) experience, the love in question already differs from parental or filial love or the love between friends. This love involves "falling in love" and then "being in love". It includes the "enchantment" which the beloved person effects on the lover. Far from being a youthful lunacy, genuine spousal love stirs us in our depths. Our heart cries out for requital. The "intentions" of union and benevolence, to be found in all real loves, find here their most insistent voice.

The great plays of Shakespeare, the music and operas of Mozart (nay, even the songs of Irving Berlin!) speak of this love, sing of it, and celebrate it in a hundred beautiful ways. This love speaks the language of humble gratitude, of yearning, of tender care for the loved one. It pleads for permanence — for eternal union even. It would shower all good things on the loved one, and avert the slightest discomfort. It gives birth to music and to joy even to contemplate the beloved, even to pronounce her name.

How are spousal love and human sex related? If atheistic evolution is true (can there be a serious theistic evolution?), there is no link. Everything is the result of chance, of random comings together, after a trillion trillion "trials", of atoms and elements of dead matter until at last, by some happy accident, life is made; and then animal life and then human life. Nothing human is especially high or noble, proceeding as it does from the random and irrational combination of material elements. Love is nothing special; nor is beauty or humility. That we humans come in different sexes means nothing: it is but the accidental result of some evolutionary twist as the atoms of matter march blindly into the future. From this point of view, sex is even something grotesque and absurd.

Not so if a personal Creator, God, is at the source of all be-

ing and all earthly life and experience. Then nothing is seen
as a result of mere chance, least of all the profound complementary character—both biological and spiritual—of the two human sexes. Von Hildebrand teaches that it is the God-willed
meaning—the destiny—of human sex to be both the bodily expression and the completion of wedded love. Love yearns for
union on all levels. Love seeks self-revelation and self-donation
to the loved one. Love is of the heart. When now the persons
freely will to share a life together, a bond is established: marriage itself. This voluntarily places the future lives of the partners beyond any arbitrariness or caprice.

Only within the garden of wedded love ought the veils that
guard our sexual secret be opened: to admit the loved one. Far
from being something peripheral or superficial, the sex of each
of us belongs to our inner sanctum. Its great personal depth
is just the reason for its lofty destiny in marriage.

By the same measure, sex isolated from wedded love constitutes the core of impurity. Von Hildebrand distinguishes
three elements of the sin of impurity. He writes:

In the first place, *I fling myself away* by giving up this personal
secret to another with no intention of a real and final surrender
to that person or of entering thus into a lasting external union
with my partner. . . .

. . . Besides this squandering of self, which may be described
as a specific *degradation* of myself and my partner, this abuse of
sex always involves a second factor, a *desecration*. To perform the
act which signifies the hallowed union of two human beings in
one flesh, and should be the expression and fulfillment of a lasting and indissoluble bond of love, with a partner to whom we
are not united by the sacred tie of matrimony is obviously a
desecration of the most awful kind. . . .

. . . Every abuse of sex further involves a specific defilement.
. . . [The] aspects which sex displays when it is isolated and
no longer "formed" from within by wedded love and the consciousness of God's sanction—namely, the siren-song of sensual
attraction with its poisonous sweetness, and diabolic evil lust—

display a peculiar power to corrupt and defile the soul. The moment any man in his employment of sex "wills" one of these two aspects, and gives himself up to it, he incurs a mysterious defilement and separates himself in an altogether unique fashion from God.[2]

All the above concerns the mystery of human sex in its "unitive" role. The mystery becomes still deeper and more beautiful when the procreative role is added. This is a topic in itself, which is linked to the great moral issue of the sin of artificial contraception. For the purposes of this paper, however, I should like to end with a final quote from von Hildebrand linking both roles: "It is no chance that God has invested the sexual act with creative significance. As God's love is the creative principle in the universe, so love is everywhere creation, and there is a profound significance in the nexus — at once symbol and reality — whereby from the creative act in which two become one flesh from love and in love, the new human being proceeds."[3]

NOTES

[1] *In Defense of Purity* (New York: Sheed & Ward, 1935), p. 14. This book has since been reprinted several times in English. A new printing is due in late fall 1989, from Franciscan University of Steubenville.

[2] Ibid., pp. 35–37.

[3] Ibid., p. 26.

MICHAEL PLATT

THE HAPPINESS OF WILLA CATHER

What would you teach your children? What stories would you tell them? What old favorites would you read them aloud? And when they can read for themselves, what books would you tell them to read and what ones would you have about for them to discover on their own? These questions, the questions of parents, are immensely consequential for their children and for the nation. Even though one can recommend the works of Willa Cather, these questions have deep roots, long histories, and no entirely easy answers.

I

Ever since the Romans were about to become Christians and the Christians were about to assume Roman political offices, thoughtful Christians and thoughtful statesmen have asked how one can be both a Christian and a statesman. Can one be a prince and a saint? A general and a bishop? A warrior and a martyr? A king and a prophet? Can one even be a gentleman and a Christian?[1] What, then, is the proper relation of the things of Caesar and the things of Christ?

Various are the answers given by Augustine, Thomas, More, Luther, Pascal, Newman, and Kierkegaard. And various also are the answers given by Dante, Richelieu, Locke, Lincoln, and Churchill. However, ever since our American colonial forefathers appealed to "Nature" and to "Nature's God" in their Declaration of Independence and went on to specify the relation of the two in their First Amendment, it has been more than possible to argue that one can be both a citizen and a Christian, that the aims of the priest and the patriot do not clash, and even that the President and the preacher might be the same man. The generation of the Framers thought it self-evident that republican government and religious liberty, understood as the liberty to practice that form of Christianity a citizen has conscientiously chosen, are mutually strengthening.

Tocqueville made the argument stronger still by pointing out to post–French Revolution adherents of throne and altar that America, without throne and without established altar, was more pious than ancient France had ever been and by simultaneously pointing out to atheist advocates of Liberty that nowhere was Liberty more enjoyed than in pious America. Coming down to the present day, some students of Tocqueville, also like him affectionate students of America, see a "Catholic moment" in America (and some of them perhaps hope for an "American moment" in the Holy Roman Church).

Certainly for those who respect the principles of the American Founding and revere the Redeeming Christ, it is essential to understand how political respect and religious reverence might cohere.[2]

The tension between citizenship and discipleship can be seen clearly in daily lives of the many Christian and patriot parents who feel responsible for their children and deliberate about their natural duty to educate them.[3] Distressed at the deleterious neglect of their children's minds and the injurious indoctrination of their children's souls in the American public school of today, in which neither country, nor good, nor God seems to have a very important place, many of these parents now find themselves considering home-schooling their own children, alone or together with other Christian families. Whether they elect to do so or not, such dutiful parents will find themselves considering a question all parents, true parents, ask themselves: What stories should I tell my children? Or read aloud to them? And later: What books should I give them to read?[4]

What you read when you are young is fateful. The boy is

the father of the man, the girl the mother of the woman. What we dream about, we become. "To fulfill the dreams of one's youth; that is the best that can happen to a man", says a priest in one of Willa Cather's novels.[5] The soul of a child yearns for heroes. To the young child, almost all adults are heroes. As children grow older, stronger, and more intelligent, they begin to distinguish among adults. They have as their heroes inventors, explorers, generals, prophets, and statesmen. For instruction they may still look to their parents, or grandparents, or some adult, perhaps some teacher in school, for such youths expect to become fathers and mothers. They read the Bible and Shakespeare, and the best youths read and reread them. They dream of being great and also expect and hope to be good. Pray for the nation that fashions, in place of such youths, "teen-agers"![6]

Growing up in America today, such youngsters (not "teen-agers") will naturally seek American heroes and Christian heroes to admire and to consider emulating. However, these children will not necessarily find a coherent pantheon of heroes to emulate. Can we guarantee that all parts of the good will cohere or that without intellectual effort the way they do cohere will be discerned? Young boys and girls in America will grow up admiring two sorts of heroes—pioneers and Christians. And young Catholic boys and girls will in addition grow up wanting to emulate priests and saints. Could there be a pioneer saint or a saintly pioneer? Could one man be both? Failing that, since there might be a separation of powers between the two, can one soul want to be both? Do these desires fit in one soul peaceably, or do they make war? Could there be a Catholic moment in America? Is there an American answer to the question of the relation of the things of Caesar and the things of Christ? For American Catholic parents, these two questions boil down to the relation of the pioneer and the saint.

In what follows, I shall address these questions by turning to two novels by Willa Cather: *My Ántonia* and *Death Comes for the Archbishop,* both about pioneers who may be saints.[7]

II. Three Pullings of the Good

More than most other writers, save perhaps Plato, Willa Cather makes the good—its nature, what it points to, and what protects it—the subject of her work. No page is without some savor of it, no loss of it without sadness, no hindering of it without indignation, and no epiphany of it without joy. You cannot read a paragraph from any of her works without being brought in touch with it. She, her characters, and her readers are always struggling to know the good better. How we come to discover it, to know it, to become it even, is her theme, and in her work the good is often the cause of more good, unto the third generation.

There are three prints of the good, like three stages in an etching, three pullings as they might be called, and *My Ántonia* shows us all three. There is first the way things are in the present, especially in the present of childhood, when everything is fresh and for the first time. Fortunate are those whose first experiences in life are on a farm, under a big sky and a warm sun, with good parents (or grandparents) who love us— that is, nurture, teach, chastise, and cheer us. Even imperfect ones will do. For the child turns to the good and avoids the bad like a sunflower seeking the sun. In a city, everything depends on humans; in the country, nature may compensate for fallen nature. Nothing in nature is finer than a fine human being, but no fineness develops in a human who is indifferent to fineness elsewhere, especially the fineness inherent in the splendid integrity of nature.

> I felt motion in the landscape; in the fresh, easy-blowing morning wind, and in the earth itself, as if the shaggy grass were a sort of loose hide, and underneath it herds of wild buffalo were galloping, galloping. . . . I wanted to walk straight on through the red grass and over the edge of the world, which could not be far away. The light air about me told me that the world ended here: only the ground and sun and sky were left, and if one went a little farther there would be only sun and sky, and one would

float off into them, like the tawny hawks which sailed over our heads making slow shadows on the grass.[8]

Thus, in this story, Jim enjoys the good in Nebraska and Ántonia enjoys it there too; together they discover it, in treks and adventures, in victories against ancient snakes, in the prairie grass, under the giant sky.

> I sat down in the middle of the garden . . . and leaned my back against a pumpkin. . . . The earth was warm under me, and warm as I crumbled it through my fingers. . . . I kept as still as I could. Nothing happened. I did not expect anything to happen. . . . I was entirely happy. Perhaps we feel like that when we die and become a part of something entire, whether it is sun and air, or goodness and knowledge. At any rate, that is happiness; to be dissolved into something complete and great.[9]

Sense and intelligence combine to connect Jim and Ántonia to that something complete and great. In learning the English tongue, she from him and he once again by teaching her, attentive to the very additions her tricky spirit brings to the language, they know the freshness that all learning brings and that makes the whole world our habitation. Jim will live his life far away from Nebraska. And part of Ántonia already lives far away from the good she first enjoyed in Bohemia. Both, not without suffering, will be sustained by the good they first enjoyed on the prairie, from which they nonetheless departed, and which they nonetheless never lost.

Then there is the second pulling, when these pristine, inexhaustible impressions of the good are shared. In this book, such a sharing takes place when Jim tells Ántonia what he never told her then: how her father's spirit seemed to dwell in their house, after his death, on his way back to Bohemia. The best, of course, are precious and therefore private, but when they are shared, with proper respect for their preciousness,[10] their good increases. Jim's story is a gift to Ántonia; it becomes precious to her. And the fact that it was precious to her makes it more precious to him.

Then there is a third pulling of the good, in which the pristine first partaking is shared with a whole new generation. We see this in Ántonia and her family, how she has shared all that was good in Jim with her family. As he goes up the driveway, he is known to the little boys and girls. More, he is loved. Even before he sees Ántonia, he knows that the bond between them has been for the good. There are no regrets in her heart, so there need not be any in his. Nothing is more thrilling in this story than seeing how the good in Ántonia, which was so special and fresh, has bloomed in her and come to fruit in her family. The gifts she always appreciated, in the fields, in the cherished memories, have been multiplied. Although this novel is not very long, it gives us the long view of life as very few others do. Wonderful as she was at sixteen, Ántonia is greater at forty than she was at sixteen. What was becoming is now being.

As you go through life, if you get to see some of the same people from time to time, you wonder how they will turn out. Reunions are the way the scattered get to satisfy this desire. Some people seem to be the same as they always were; they could not go far and did not, but they did keep to what they were. A few surprise us; they surpass themselves; perhaps we did not know them. Others might have been so much more; their gifts were evident, their desires high, the range of what they might have become immense. They and chance chose, and one sees the consequences. Is it not true that very few turned out well? In comparison with what they were as children, what they have become as adults is inferior — not in accomplishments, in competencies, or in skills, perhaps, but in their vital core.

Thus, in this novel, Tiny Soderball is less as a competent, self-assured, wealthy woman than she was as a skipping girl; Lena is less as an elegant, companionable lady than she was as a weary girl seeking solitude with the animals and securing it in her Saturday-night bath. Even Ántonia and Jim are not quite what we desire them to be. We wonder whether they should have made a marriage. All through the story, knowing the title, we wonder in what sense Ántonia will one day be Jim's "*my* Ántonia". Then when she returns seduced, abandoned by Donovan, yet firm in her love of her child, we hope that Jim will marry her. It does not happen. What are we to think of this incompleteness? What did Ántonia think then? At their parting, Jim said he would be back. We hoped soon. Did Ántonia hope soon? By the time he comes back, twenty years have passed. Whatever she felt at first, she, we understand, does not regret a thing, and that releases Jim. He sees that she is battered but undiminished. Now he sets to writing all the story. He could not have done it before seeing this point in it.

And this is the fourth impression, or pulling of the good: the story of Ántonia and Jim or, for short, *My Ántonia,* in which all the first three pullings of the good are included and all shared with people who will, unlike Ántonia's children, never meet the characters in person. Yet is it any wonder that they might want to? I understand that some readers go to Nebraska to visit the grave of the "real Ántonia".[11] It must be a grave like the one made for Ántonia's father, carved out of a country square, causing the road to bend a little, with a cross to mark it, and pristine prairie grass still growing all around it. Perfectly understandable. A perfect tribute to Ántonia and to Willa Cather, who discerned her goodness in at least four ways. Short of revelation, this fourth impression is the closest we come to knowing that the soul is immortal. All of Willa Cather's people — Neighbor Rosicky, Cecille, Archbishop Latour, Claude, Thea, Mrs. Harris, Nancy — become more translucent as their lives transpire; it is as if a light behind a stained-glass figure grew stronger, making the figure ever clearer, as the light grows brighter. Often that light grows brighter for her people themselves; the deaths of Claude, of Frontenac, and of Bishop Latour are completions of life and of earthly understanding. All might say, "That is happiness; to be dissolved into something complete and great", as the gravestone of Willa Cather in Jaffrey, New Hampshire, says. Looking back from this vantage, we realize that everything wonderful in Cather's books is written from the point of view of a loving eternity. What is was first loved and ever shall be.

It is perfectly understandable, then, why people who read Willa Cather go to visit her grave and the graves of her characters. It is also perfectly understandable why one loves to reread her books. Everyone who visits a graveyard does so for a simple reason, which we are chary of admitting: to find some dead person. That is also why we reread a good story, one with persons in it who are that unique mixture of soul and body, for whom the earth was created and who will perdure it. We believe in such ghosts and sometimes, in a moment of self-knowledge, see that we ourselves are such ghosts in bodies.

This belief has nothing to do with the worship of art. Indeed, one of the most important qualities of Willa Cather's work is that in it there are real people who like to read a good book, who know what a difference in life good books can make, who yearn for the good that a good book has discovered to them, and who will make the search for that good a habit of a lifetime. Thus, in *The Professor's House* we have Tom Outland studying his Virgil in the Southwest desert, and in *My Ántonia* we have Jim making the same Virgil the path to college. In what other author does one witness what college can mean to an untutored, desiring heart? Upon discovering the world of ideas, Jim in *My Ántonia* says, "when one first enters that world everything else fades for a time, and all that went before it as if it had not been." With her peculiar clarity, Ántonia once told him, "It must make you very happy, Jim, to have fine thoughts like that in your mind all the time, and to have words to put them in. I always wanted to go to school, you know."

Willa Cather is the most teacherly writer there has ever been, save Plato; she is always looking for sparks of virtue, honorable ambition, and real excellence in people. Her insight finds them everywhere, in rich variety—evil is far more often dull, even to itself, than good is—and her charity finds noble sparks in many of the frail, old, or immature; she has a special eye for the gifted, for how far they might go, and how far they will have to. Again and again, she writes of the impediments that oppose gifted youngsters, how their virtue overcomes them and how, by growing strong, they become who they were meant to be by nature. Willa Cather's years of teaching in Lincoln and Pittsburgh, and her years of teaching herself before, during, and after, were never an impediment to her writing. In her writing, she always favors those who can see beautiful, true, good things; she was a teacher through and through, and was always looking for her superior in heart and in mind. Yet, important as teaching is, she knew that it never succeeds where the teacher forgets that all important learning is self-learning. Thus, important as Thea's teachers are in *The Song of the Lark,* none is as essential as the great learner Thea herself.

The great lesson of the heart, of how the most important qualification in life is desire, is summed up in the scene in *My Ántonia* where a blind child, blind from birth, climbs in an open window and makes his way to the piano, whose melodies he has been secretly hearing, and, despite his fear of a whipping, starts to play the keys he has never touched before. Nor do they refuse his ardor:

Through the dark Samson found his way to the Thing, to its mouth. He touched it softly, and it answered softly, kindly. He shivered and stood still. Then he began to feel it all over, ran his finger-tips along the slippery sides, embraced the carved legs, tried to get some conception of its shape and size, of the space it occupied in primeval night. It was cold and hard, and like nothing else in his black universe. He went back to its mouth, began at one end of the keyboard and felt his way down into the mellow thunder, as far as he could go. He seemed to know that it must be done with the fingers, not with the fists or the feet. He approached this highly artificial instrument through a mere instinct, and coupled himself to it, as if he knew it was to piece him out and make a whole creature of him. After he had tried over all the sounds, he began to finger out passages from things Miss Nellie had been practising, passages that were already his, that lay under the bone of his pinched, conical little skull, definite as animal desires.[12]

It is as a teacher in another of Willa Cather's novels says: "A man can do anything if he wishes enough. . . . Desire is creation, is the magical element in that process. If there were an instrument by which to measure desire, one could foretell achievement."[13]

Just as anyone who hates speech, who despises the word, should be invited to read Helen Keller's story of the day she discovered all at once the intelligibility of the world and the equal miracle that this intelligibility can be shared—and then she was no longer angry—so anyone who doubts the beauty of music, whom music mads, should be invited to read this episode in *My Ántonia*.[14] And anyone doubting the bounty of the good in our suffering world might be invited to read both, I suppose.

My Ántonia is primarily about the good, about the good as seen in peace and in a good mother. The scenes in which we see this are wonderful. First we see it in the children, their good manners, their direct gazes, the way they know Jim because they have been told good stories about him—he is already an "Uncle" to them—and their affectionate respect for their parents, especially their mother. After a lapse of twenty years, she looks this way to Jim:

> She was a battered woman now, not a lovely girl; but she still had that something which fires the imagination, could still stop one's breath for a moment by a look or gesture that somehow revealed the meaning in common things. She had only to stand in the orchard, to put her hand on a little crab tree and look up at the apples, to make you feel the goodness of planting and tending and harvesting at last. All the strong things of her heart came out in her body, that had been so tireless in serving generous emotions.
>
> It was no wonder that her sons stood tall and straight. She was a rich mine of life, like the founders of early races.[15]

It is wonderful to see how the good in Ántonia, which we first enjoyed in her as a girl, has grown and become so fruitful. The role of fathers in defending the good from evil is not emphasized in *My Ántonia*. There is so much good in the book, in its lovely heroine and in the family life centered around her, that one might be tempted to believe there can be families without countries; that rural paradise — or what Plato's Glaukon calls "sow city" — in which everybody lives simple, healthy, peaceful, and just, without ever having to be just to each other, or to enemies, by defending their country, is possible. It is not so, and Willa Cather knows it.

Becoming a mother means for Ántonia being no longer able to kill something; even to make merry at the visit of an old friend, she cannot bring herself to wring the neck of a fatted chicken. This reluctance is right, right for Ántonia and for many other mothers; it is right to be reluctant, although it would not be right to refuse or oppose. Ántonia knows this when she acknowledges that her great failing was not being able to acknowledge evil in anyone she loved. This weakness made her slavish to her brutal brother, got her into trouble with greasy-whiskered Mr. Cutter, and allowed her to be seduced and abandoned by a smooth jerk. How fortunate that her good husband is good! This she now understands. She cannot bring herself to shoot anything now, might be tempted to forbid her children to play with guns, but she knows better. Where there are humans, there will be vices — which means that other humans will have to be on guard, risk killing and being killed, to smite the wicked and hinder evil.[16]

Ántonia might have known this earlier, as Willa Cather does. There is first of all Jim's killing of the large snake. Had Ántonia remembered that there are snakes, even in the paradisiac prairie, let alone in town, she might have suffered less and visited less suffering on others — for example, Jim, who gets caressed by the oily, whiskered, lecherous Cutter, and then bashed black and blue. Augustine says, "Hate the sin and love the sinner." Without disagreeing, Cather says, "Forgive the sin but oppose the sinner."

III. Bishop, Statesman, Saint

After the Mexican War, with the vast oceans away from Europe, and with the vast British navy to clear them, and after the Civil War, when slavery was forever forbidden advancement, America was free to civilize the West, to go from sea to shining sea, spreading the fruits of peace, with land for families to work, own, and enjoy. America was so free that it would have been possible to forget the necessity of war and preparation for war, to believe that there could be families without countries, that there could be women like Ántonia and children like hers without statesmen like Lincoln or generals like Grant. But Willa Cather did not forget these things. In peace and isolation, the soul often rejoices in the good, but isolationism is irresponsible.[17]

In another of her novels, she treats us to the discovery of peace in the form of the Mesa Verde dwelling place. Here, high into the side of a cliff, protected by a strong river and a narrow pass, a lone cowboy discovers an Indian city. No one has been to this beautiful city in 368 years. We agree wholly with the narrator's wish never to leave this peaceful place and also with the priest who suggests that the peculiar towers must be for stellar observation. Here, the priest goes on to say, these people, at first rude and barbarous, though farmers, must have begun to cultivate the arts of peace. Those arts are wonderful, but Cather never forgets the probable end of these peaceful people; protected by their natural fort, too protected, they are one day slain, every one of them, by some rude, unruly people happening upon them while they cultivate their fields across the river. Nor does the narrator, Tom Outland, forget. When America enters World War I, its peaceful shipping having been subjected to the unrestricted submarine attacks of Ludendorff's total Germany, Tom signs up.

Although Willa Cather thought it made sense to live your life for something greater than your country, she did not think it is foolish to die for your country.[18] Claude Wheeler and his mother in *One of Ours* follow the battle of the Marne as if it were happening in North Dakota. Although Claude dies in the futile trench slaughter of the Western Front, neither his life nor the cause of his country is futile. Although Cather appreciates the fact that Woodrow Wilson's idealism is something different from the good we should have been fighting for, that does not mean the two do not overlap considerably. And it does not mean that the good of the individual soldier is lost in service to country. In his death, Claude not only shows courage and loyalty, risking himself for others, but on the way to it finds something he always wanted, inarticulately and awkwardly, but would never have found without the war. Claude and his mother cringe at the rape of Belgium and understand the battle of the Marne as a struggle to protect civilization, but when Claude gets to France, he gets to understand what civilization is. Although "mediocred" by his family and town more than himself, in truth Claude is mediocre, awkward, his choices in life — such as his wife, Enid — too accidental. It is a wonder that we care so much for him, but we do, and we rejoice, with him, that he is going to war. There on the Western Front, in France, he finds the higher satisfaction he has dimly sought all his life, in a comrade who plays violin, in the French way of eating, with a delicious meal that is but a background to conversation, and in the rose window of the Church of St. Ouen in Rouen which he wanders into, all before he dies, more satisfied than he has ever been in his life. Service to country, even unto death, also rewards the soul.

A further proof lies in Willa Cather's novel *Death Comes for the Archbishop*. The good man who stands at the center of this Christian story is no pacifist. Early in his service on the way to Santa Fé, stopping at a hovel, he and his vicar are warned by a terrified woman to flee the cunning host, but they do not just slip away. Drawing a pistol he has carried for just such encounters, Father Latour makes the malefactor appreciate that he means business, and when he reaches the civil authorities, he sends them to apprehend the man and save the wretched wife. It is precisely at this point in his apostolic service that Latour meets Kit Carson; their mutual regard and alliance represent a harmony of the civil and the ecclesiastical powers; the established American government and the unestablished Church want things that can not only coexist but support each other.

Not that the pistol-packing priest is a trigger-happy, violent man or even a practiced warrior. If need be, he is ready to defend himself and the innocent with weapons, but wherever he can, he will turn to the civil authority. Shane he is not; the pistol he draws on the villain Scales has no dry powder, although Father Joseph's does. In sum, this archbishop is a statesman. Arriving at a diocese long untended, he knows which evils and evildoers to remove immediately, whatever the popular fuss (Father Gallengos), and which ones to wait out patiently, only seeming to condone (Padre Martinez). *Festina lente*. The quality of the prudence that works in the scope of an archbishopric is evident in a good work accomplished long before Archbishop Latour reaches Santa Fé. Back in Auvergne when a young man, Father Latour watched his future vicar, Father Vaillant, nearly torn apart by his vow to become God's missionary and his reluctance to leave his parents' house; with the sound of the approaching coach in their ears, Father Latour improvises a solution: come along to Paris, and if you still feel this way, we will ask the bishop to release you from your vow. It is a perfect stroke; at that moment to tell his troubled friend, however gently, "you must decide" would have split him in two parts that might never have been put back together.

If Archbishop Latour is a statesman, he is also a Christian man. Not only does he recognize superior spiritual gifts in others, in his indefatigable vicar and in the long-suffering Sada, but he has some of them himself. His heart leaps to see a cruciform juniper in the place where he discovers Hidden Water and the lost community living around it discovers him; in this he sees the same Hand that guided the prophet of the Children of Israel. When Father Latour sees that he has some hard decision to make, he retires, into mediation and solitude, seeking it now in his chapel and now in a solitary, wind-encircled hogan. His day begins in prayer; his daily works are prayers in action, and so are his long designs. Archbishop Latour enjoys the world, but gravely, always gracious but never warm, good to all yet known to few; that his favorite author is Pascal fits something in this temper.[19]

Yet, like Cicero and his Scipio in his *De Re Publica,* this statesman heading for eternity is much concerned with friendship. The friendship of Ishmael and Queequeg exists more to make a Melvillian point than to enjoy anything more important than a pipe; the friendship of Huck and Tom is all play, that of Huck and Jim, although it is just, brave, and loving, is no more substantial than the bonds of boys out of school for summer. By contrast, the friendship of Father Latour and Father Vaillant is mature and full and lasting; it combines civil pleasures, thoughtful inquiries, and shared good works. Work and calling unite these friends and also divide them. Together they set out to serve God and his creatures in the vast Southwest. Together they proceed; together they succeed step by step. Without the directness of the one and the courtesy of the other, Madame Isabella Olivares would never have sacrificed her vanity in court and delivered the willed wealth of her husband so that the archbishop's cathedral might be built. Jean is the more contemplative; Joseph, the more active. Joseph's motto is "rest in action"; Jean's might be "through action to rest". Neither would be so fine without some of the other's dominant virtue.[20]

Yet the same Voice that brought these two so complementary souls together for work then separates them for more work when he calls Father Vaillant away to Utah and Colorado. The only important mistake, perhaps sin, that Father Latour ever commits is to call his dear vicar away from his work west of Santa Fé, but this mistake is reversed and even perhaps justified and redeemed by his ready acceptance of Father Vaillant's subsequent call to Colorado. Contendo and Angelica, the fine pair of white mules, should not be separated, but this fine pair of priests needs must be. The friendship of Jean Marie Latour and Joseph Vaillant is lifelong and, if their faith be true, may not cease with death.

Death Comes for the Archbishop is also about death, about how death comes for Archbishop Latour, about how he came to death, and about how his whole life was a preparation for death. No other American novel I know of, save others by Willa Cather, such as *My Mortal Enemy* and *The Professor's House,* presents such a preparation. There is plenty of death in Hawthorne and Melville, in Poe and James, and in Hemingway and Fitzgerald, but none that anyone prepares for. Death is violent or accidental, sickly or swift, but in any case not anticipated, awaited, prepared for. Nor are the last words of these representative American men and women memorable.[21]

Willa Cather shows us that Archbishop Latour dies of having lived. As death comes for him, he has chosen to meet it in Santa Fé, rather than, as others and even he himself expected, in his native Auvergne. In the Southwest, death weighs less heavily on a man; there it is always morning, the air fragrant with sagebrush, light and vivacious. "Something soft and wild and free, something that whispered to the ear on the pillow, lightened the heart, softly, softly picked the lock, slid the bolts, and released the prisoned spirit of man into the wind, into the blue and gold, into the morning, into the morning!"[22]

Moreover, the Southwest is for the archbishop the scene of his life's work. On his way to death, he is more conscious of the whole pageant of his life, especially his great friendship with Father Vaillant, than of the present; as he approaches death, all scenes of the past are equipresent to him; he sees time as

God does. "He was soon to have done with calendared time, and it had already ceased to count for him. He sat in the middle of his own consciousness; none of his former states of mind were lost or outgrown. They are all within reach of his hand, and all comprehensible."[23]

Yet when he returns to the present, to speak with Bernard, to greet Eusabio the Navaho, or to move back to his study at Santa Fé, he sees the lovely countryside, which he trusts will always endure, and the human scene, so transformed by his own apostolic labors, so threatened perhaps by future progress but, so he also trusts, worthy of the same loving support he has received from the Creator. This man has so lived that the coming of death is for him a not entirely unwelcome visitation. Death completes his life. His tomb—the cathedral he built for his diocese, from local stone in a Romanesque form brought from his native southern France—will be his gift to every future diocesan soul and as such, only as such, a monument to himself.

One of the things that gives Father Latour most pleasure as he lies dying is the unusual justice of a government. Most unjustly had the American government forced the noble Navahos to vacate their native lands, especially that green bastion of civility the Canyon de Chelly, where they were at last done in, by Latour's for-once-misguided friend Kit Carson. The destruction of these Indians might have meant the destruction of nature, for they have "none of the European's desire to 'master' nature, to arrange and re-create. They spend their ingenuity . . . in accommodating themselves to the scene. . . . It was the Indian's way to pass through a country without disturbing anything; to pass and leave no trace, like fish through the water or birds through the air."[24] The mystery of Jacinto's cave is safe with the courteous Christian who thinks these thoughts.

Yet despite all likelihood, the American government admits its mistake and restores the Indians to their native lands. In recognizing civility, these Americans qualify as civil, however belatedly. These dry ancestral lands mean more to the Navaho than almost anything. The lands are at once the basis of these Indians' shepherding way of life and the object of their religious reverence; they cannot exist elsewhere, take up new ways, go into a distant land, sojourn in Egypt, or labor among the Moabites. Their gods are fixed and fix them. Father Latour not only recognizes this, thinks their cause just, but blesses them and their affection, however fixed and primal.

That he does so is all the more remarkable when we consider that he, although he loves his native Auvergne, not only accepts the call of God to voyage to America, journey to Ohio, and later trek to New Mexico, supping on thin imitations of his beloved French soups, but chooses to die in Santa Fé rather than in the region of his nativity. The Creator God he is guided by not only blesses each earthly place with peculiar beauties, but being the God of all peoples, calls many to pilgrim forth to foreign lands; and, being the God of all the earth, is not unhappy to send death to his servant in a foreign land, and also smiles upon him for succoring those whose reverence for the Creator is focused on one place and one place only. Although Willa Cather never says that Archbishop Latour is a saint, she suggests a great deal that might make one ask, as he never would, whether he is one.

Whether patronizing or cozy, the characterization of Willa Cather as a regional author is quite mistaken. That she loved regions, many of them, from Nebraska to Avignon,[25] is true, and that there is an intelligent patriotism in her work is also true, if now unappreciated. But she loves human beings more than regions, and she understands them as souls, not selfs, because she loves eternity more than all. She speaks of being absorbed in something great, but her happiness was to be absorbed in the greatest something, and in such a way that all the lesser things in the plenteously good created whole were properly loved, especially really good souls, God's best images.

That whole includes the current state of divided and subdivided Christendom. If a Christian were asked to point to the books in American literature that portray a good Christian —

someone of whom one might say, "Yes, that is a portrait; that is the sort of soul I aspire to be" — there are no better portraits than those in the novels of Willa Cather, and few competitors.[26] That these portraits are most notably of Catholics should give food for thought to Protestants, and that they are written by one who never ceased to profess herself an Episcopalian ought to give thought to Catholics. Perhaps C. S. Lewis might resolve whatever is perplexing in this fact by remarking, "I too wrote as a mere Christian."[27]

NOTES

[1] See Karl Löwith, "Can There Be a Christian Gentleman?" *Nature, History, and Existentialism* (Evanston, Ill.: Northwestern University Press, 1966), pp. 204–13.

[2] And for Catholic Christians it is acutely essential, for we look to the Holy See for guidance and even commands in a way that few Protestants look to a foreign principality or prince.

[3] What Thomas calls a part of the natural law shared with the animals seems nearly denied as a parental right by state attempts to regulate or hinder home schooling. Christians may take comfort in the fact that Christ is the most notable example of a home-schooled child there ever has been.

[4] The best sources of counsel and advice I know of are John Senior's *The Restoration of Christian Culture* (San Francisco: Ignatius Press, 1983) and the many books of Mary Pride.

[5] Father Vaillant to Father Latour in Willa Cather's *Death Comes for the Archbishop* (New York: Knopf, 1927), p. 261.

[6] Only since parents in the 1950s in the West began orphaning their children to television, rock music, and drugs have young people grown up without admiring some adult or wishing to become one. Before World War II, there were no "teenagers". Compare the entries in Webster II and Webster III or spend a rainy day looking through old *Life* magazines; in that faraway time, there were youths. The highest ambition of the teenager is to become a more perfect teenager, perhaps a rock-and-drug star, a movie star, or a personality, some slick version of the teenager's own vices. See my review-essay on Allan Bloom's *Closing of the American Mind*, entitled "Souls Without Longing", especially section IV, in *Interpretation*, xviii, 3, Spring, 1991, and my essay "The Teenager and the West", forthcoming somewhere, I hope.

[7] This essay is a portion of a much longer one, growing toward a book, entitled "Nature and Nature's God", which treats the *Ur*-Western, Owen Wister's *The Virginian,* and much else, including the Declaration, Tocqueville, and Lincoln. I would like to thank the Wethersfield Foundation for the opportunity to deliver a version of this essay at Marymount College in New York City, fifty paces from my boyhood home. The snowballs with which I, along with my friends, pelted the girls of this Catholic college every snowfall were, I now believe, inspired with an ardor and directed by a divinely accurate aim, the true target of which only many a year later was graciously disclosed.

[8] *My Ántonia* (Boston: Houghton Mifflin, 1918), p. 16.

[9] Ibid., p. 18.

[10] As, for example, when Pierre and Natasha in *War and Peace* share the as-yet untold-to-anyone stories of their suffering.

[11] Her name is Anna Pavelka (1869–1955); she was born Anna Sadilek in Missovic, Bohemia, and is buried on the treeless prairie north of Red Cloud, Nebraska.

[12] *My Ántonia*, p. 187.

[13] *The Professor's House* (New York: Knopf, 1925), p. 29.

[14] In the *Politics*, Aristotle says that the person who lives outside the *polis* (or political community) must be either a beast or a god, and that he will ever be making war. Thus, the first lesson little Helen, who had become a tyrant through her parents' pampering, had to learn was obedience. Only then did she trust her teacher, Anne Sullivan, soon after W-A-T-E-R, and take what Socrates would call "the second sailing".

[15] *My Ántonia*, p. 353.

[16] Although the American polity has enshrined the right to bear arms in the militia as among the rights that protect and, for many, define self-government, it has also long recognized the conscientious aversion to bearing arms as a just excuse from doing so. But it has not recognized a selective right to do so — not only, as the Supreme Court has ruled (*Gillette v. United States* and *Negre v. Larson*, 1971), because it would be hard to have an army but also because in a democracy the proper place to object selectively is in politics, through persuading your fellow voters, supporting candidates you agree with, or running for office yourself.

[17] On the way, America came to misunderstand its own Monroe Doctrine, its tacit alliance with the British Navy during the nineteenth century, and after it acquired an interest in the Philippines, it also misunderstood the necessity of increasing its power to match its responsibility and thus contributed not a little to two world wars and their consequences. See Walter Lippmann, *U.S. Foreign Policy: Shield of the Republic* (New York: Pocket Books, 1943).

[18] I appropriate a remark of C. S. Lewis'.

[19] In *Shadows on the Rock,* even as she admires the nobility of the nun Jeanne Le Ber, Willa Cather criticizes her: Jeanne gave hurt to her father by living as a shut-in and she was wrong to say "No, I will not go with you" to the good Pierre Charron. Stealing into her church one night and overhearing her wretched voice, Pierre is finally sure that she was wrong and that her wrong choice means he should have no regrets. Choosing wrong means that you are wrong. Willa Cather seems to believe that the wholly cloistered life is not a calling. The pattern of Christ, with its intermittent solitude and teaching, would dictate something closer to the lives of Latour and Vaillant and Thea Kronberg, with their service, denial, and suffering, alternately *activa* and *contemplativa*.

[20] These types receive extreme portraits in Thea in *The Song of the Lark* and Ántonia in *My Ántonia*. Between the artist and the mother there is no middle, mixed choice, Cather seems to suggest.

[21] See *Death Comes for the Archbishop*, p. 170, for remarks on this theme. In

the novel, there is also the prepared death of the miserly Padre Lucero and the lustful Padre Martinez.

22 *Death Comes for the Archbishop*, p. 276.

23 Ibid., p. 290.

24 Ibid., pp. 233–34.

25 The novel she was working on when she died was set in Avignon in the thirteenth century.

26 Perhaps Lena in Faulkner's *Light in August* or Dilsey in *The Sound and the Fury*. I have asked friends for other examples, and what they say suggests that, however Christian the perspective of Walker Percy or Flannery O'Connor, there are no good Christians in their work, only seedy or grotesque ones, respectively, vessels of Christian discovery perhaps but not patterns of Christian virtue.

27 Judging from her high school graduation speech, "Superstition and Investigation", in which she contrasts scientific enlightenment with religious obscurity, the girl who dissected animals and at college still intended to be a doctor traveled a long way to become the author of *My Ántonia* and *Death Comes for the Archbishop*, albeit a circular way considering that she had always loved the Ántonia she met on first coming into the Plains country. Simone Weil might say, "All school studies diligently pursued are a preparation for prayer."